D1475069

SAN FRANCISCO'S BEST DIVE BARS

by Todd Dayton

Photographs by Greg Roden

GAMBLE GUIDES

Ig Publishing

San Francisco's Best Dive Bars
© 2004 by Todd Dayton
All Rights Reserved
Printed in Canada

Published by Gamble Guides
Gamble Guides is an imprint of Ig Publishing
178 Clinton Avenue
Brooklyn, NY 11205
www.igpub.com
igpublishing@earthlink.net

ISBN: 0-9703125-8-X

10 9 8 7 6 5 4 3 2 1

Book Interior design by Dayna Navaro
Maps © by reineckandreineck

This book would not have been possible without the efforts of a number of people who threw caution and the health of their livers to the wind — Krump, DJ Gravy, Boogie, Boris, Greg, Pumpkin, Campbell, Justin, Bret, Ms. Ober, Dr. Youssof, Meredith, Derek, Lena, and, of course, Mom.

Dedicated to Arthur — I really hope you get that downtown job tomorrow.

Introduction

On a recent visit, my favorite Tenderloin nightspot, once a haven for ornery and inebriated old codgers, had been overrun by the vapidly cheery and oh-so-beautiful set, sipping Cosmos and chatting on their cell phones. It was all I could do to get my lips around a bottle of Bud for the lack of breathing room. As I stood tightly pressed between a pair of Gavin Newsom wanna-bes and drank my lonely beer, I thought of times past and pondered the fate of the dive bar.

During the economic high times that San Francisco experienced a few years back, a fair number of dives remade themselves with new paint, attempts at decoration, and a red candle on every table, even offering DJ nights to woo the hipster set. Other places, onetime hangouts for hustlers and pimps, veterans and losers, and yes, you and me, underwent total transformations, via new names, new music, new faces, and most importantly, new prices. And a cover charge, for god's sake.

Talking with friends about our favorite dives, I would hear a dozen times, "Oh yeah, that place used to be a real dive, but have you seen it lately?" or, "I used to love that asstrap, but these days . . ."

The bad news is that we're stuck with a glut of red-candle bars and their weekend DJs. But the aluminum foil lining to that gloomy cloud is that no matter how hard they try to paint them over, no matter how many appletinis they pour, no matter how loudly they spin those down-tempo grooves, real dives are here to stay.

A trip to many of SF's lower-end watering holes finds that these delightfully dingy establishments remain popular with the one-toothed crowd and those who love them. As a matter of fact, recent excursions to some of the happening spots of yesteryear suggest that the fate of the fading-star bar is next year's favorite dive.

I won't make any predictions about how dives will fare during the next spike in this boom-and-bust town. I'll just raise a cracked mug to the survivors that are contained within these alcohol-soaked pages.

What makes a bar a dive?

Ask a dozen people that question and you get thirteen different answers, all with the common denominator that dives are like pornography: hard to define, but you know it when you see it.

For me, the ideal dive is run by a beefy guy named Frank, where the aroma of yesterday's beer still hangs in the air, and your quest for a clean bathroom (or toilet paper, for that matter) will go eternally unanswered. A bottle of Bud costs two bucks, a shot of Jack, $3, and Pabst Blue Ribbon is served in a can. The sign outside says Steaks, Dinners, Cocktails — but there hasn't been food served since FDR was president. The prevailing decorative elements are red Naugahyde, wood-toned Formica, and cinder blocks. A couple of semi-psychotic regulars hold court on weeknights, and on weekends it's anyone's guess as to whether graveyard-level somnambulism or fever-pitch craziness will ensue. Of course, no place like this really exists in post-gold-rush San Francisco (or does it?).

The bars in this book have been chosen for a multitude of sinful reasons, the holy trinity of which are cheap prices, a strong pour, and a no-frills atmosphere. Other important factors are the presence of some stodgy old weeknight regulars, quality shit-talk from the bartenders, and the likelihood that something amazing/terrible/inexplicable could happen at any moment. I've done my best to steer clear of DJs, cover charges, or an overabundance of hipsters in cool hats and trendy eyewear.

While San Francisco's outer neighborhoods contain countless spots that are no doubt local institutions of the most ill-reputed variety, I've tried to include only those far-flung places that one might come across in the normal course of being a San Franciscan, or establishments that are well worth the effort of getting there.

All that aside, the rules of dive bars aren't much different from those for any other bar: Buy your drinking buddies a round when you can afford it, tip your bartender whether you can afford it or not, and don't pass up the jukebox. And most importantly, always empty your drink.

A note about smoking

Smoking in bars (and nearly everywhere else) is illegal in the state of California. With very few exceptions, when you light up after ordering a drink in San Francisco, you open the door to fines for yourself, your bar, and your favorite bartender. The issue has divided patrons, bar owners, law enforcement, and health officials. Some organizations have even taken out advertisements offering hot lines where do-gooders can report smoky bars.

That said, nicotine-addicted drinkers are likely to come across bars where they can indulge their vice with the encouragement and participation of bartenders and owners. Those who frequent such establishments will notice that "smoking" bars become no-smoking bars on a regular basis, and vice versa. On a random Tuesday night, for example, a place where you've never been allowed to smoke may suddenly be stocked with ashtrays and Darwin Award candidates just like in the good old days.

In most cases, I've decided to not name names and to leave the smoking issue for the bars and their customers to resolve among themselves. I'd rather not give zealous health advocates a who's who of places to send the cops.

Triple Play: What it is, where it's at, and why it's still around

Observant and far-traveling bar crawlers will notice a curious old pinball machine at odd spots around town, and even more curiously, a gray-haired old-timer plunking coin after coin into it. A quick glance at the display will reveal no flippers, just a bunch of holes and what seems like a game whose entertainment value has long since been eclipsed by new-fangled pinball machines.

But one has to explore the annals of pinball history to understand why Triple Play is still taking up precious real estate in some bars. You see, back in the 1930s and '40s, when pinball's precursors were born, the machines were basically made for gambling. They evolved to skirt anti-gambling legislation, eventually producing bingo pinballs like 1955's Triple Play, and the far less common Show Boat. You couldn't win a cash payout from the machine, only free games. But if you decided you didn't want to play your free games on the machine, you could often get the bartender to pay out.

According to some knowledgeable bingo pinball folks, San Francisco was the only place in California where one could indulge in such hardened criminal activity back in the proto-pinball heyday. Hands-on historians, however, still can. The basic premise is bingo — you sink the balls into numbered holes, and those numbers light up on the bingo board. Additional coins give you more bingo boards, and more coins increase your odds of winning. While modern gamers (or even the Pac-Man generation) will find the excitement pretty pale, these games still have a cultish following among those who played them back in the day. As for whether your bartender will pay out any free games you win, you'll need to ask (quietly).

Bacchus Kirk
Expansion Bar
Grassland
Jack's Club
Rich's Club 93

RIP —
A fond farewell to dives no more

7-11 Club
The Boondocks
The Chameleon
The Charleston
The Deuces
Doc's Clock
Gina's
Hob Nob
The Hunter
Shotwell 59
Tunnel Top

Dive ratings

The bars in this book are rated from 1 to 10:

1 ⚫

Your mom is welcome here.

5 ⚫⚫⚫⚫⚫

You can leave your bodyguard at home, but you may want to bring the pepper spray.

10 ⚫⚫⚫⚫⚫⚫⚫⚫⚫⚫

Concealed weapons recommended!

San Francisco's ten best dives
(in alphabetical order)

The Brown Jug
Sets the standard for dive living (or dying).

Expansion Bar
A low-key Market Street hideaway where cheap drinks rule.

Ha-Ra
No-bullshit drinking at one of the TL's longtime champs.

Li Po
Chinatown at its worst. Yes!

Mr. Lee-Ona's
This straight-friendly gay bar puts the loin back in the Tenderloin.

Murio's Trophy Room
If your trophy wife were a dive bar.

Nap's Only
An Outer Mission gold mine for great times and terrible karaoke.

Overflo
Men in uniform welcome.

Treat Street
Treat yourself to the city's best neighborhood bar (sorry, couldn't resist).

Uptown
The Mission's answer to turning your living room into a dive bar.

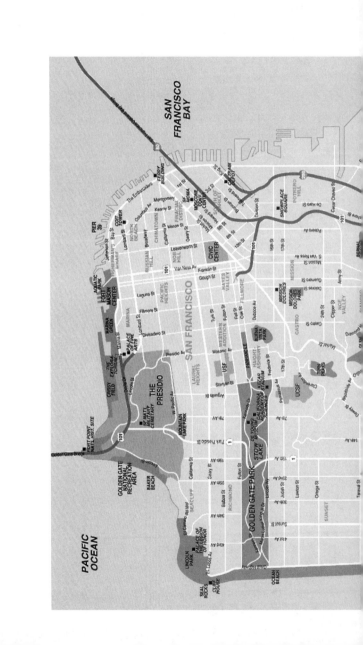

SAN FRANCISCO'S BEST DIVE BARS
(arranged by neighborhood)

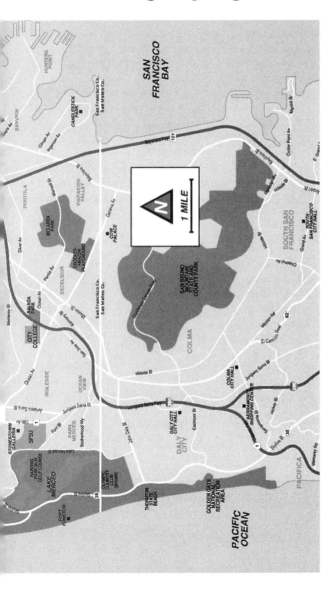

CASTRO

Expansion Bar
Lucky 13
The Transfer

CHINATOWN/NORTHBEACH

Budda Lounge
Columbus Cafe
Crow Bar
Grant & Green
Grassland
Hawaii West
The Hungry I
Kennedys
La Rocca's
    Corner
Li Po
Mr. Bing's
Red's Place
Spec's
Vieni Vieni
    Lucky Spot

HAIGHT/WESTERN ADDITION

Chances
Club Waziema
Finnegan's
    Wake
Fulton Street
The Gold Cane
John Murio's
    Trophy
    Room
Molotov's
Peacock Lounge
Trax

THE MISSION/BERNAL HEIGHTS

500 Club
3300 Club
Amnesia
The Attic
Carlos Club
Clooney's
Doc's Clock
Double Play
Dover Club
El Amigo
Il Pirata
Jack's Club
Jay & Bee
Kilowatt
LaRondalla
Latin American
    Club
Mission Bar
Nap's Only
The Odeon
Phone Booth
Rite Spot Café
Sadie's Flying
    Elephant
Thieves Tavern
Treat Street
Uptown
Wild Side West
Zeitgeist

NOB HILL/UNION SQUARE

Bacchus Kirk
C Bobby's Owl
    Tree
Chelsea Place
Overflo
Summer Place
Yong San
    Lounge

RICHMOND

The Hearth
McKenzie's Bar
Pat O'Shea's
    Mad Hatter
Trad'r Sam
Would You
    Believe?
    Cocktails

SOMA

Annie's
    Cocktail
    Lounge
Cassidy's
Dave's
Eagle's Drift-In
Red's Java
    House
Rich's Club 93

SUNSET/WEST PORTAL/PARKSIDE

Grandma's
    Saloon
Miraloma Club
The Old Rogue
Portals Tavern
Sand Bar
Shannon Arms
Silver Spur
TK's

TENDERLOIN

The Brown Jug
Club 501
Edinburgh
    Castle
Gangway
Hanaro
Ha-Ra Club
Harrington's
    Harry Pub
High Tide
Kimo's
Mr. Lee-Ona's
    Cocktail
    Lounge
Nite Cap
Route 101
Tommy's Joynt
XS

CASTRO

Take me home: Pickup spots

Expansion Bar

2124 Market St. (at Church St.)
415-863-4041

San Francisco Municipal Railway (Muni): F, J, K, L, M, N, 22, 35, 37

This is the real deal. Looking good won't get you anywhere. Looking awful won't set you back. Though from time to time the Expansion serves as a reluctant overflow zone for Café du Nord and Lucky 13 claustrophobes, it's generally true to the purpose. Cheap drinks, no pretense, conversation optional — unless you're talking with yourself. The beer revolution hasn't hit here yet, and it's not likely to. You'll find Anchor Steam in the bottle, but no microbrew on tap. No beer on tap at all.

A well-worn oak bar stretches the length of the narrow room, and it's clear this is a place with history. On the back wall is a 1944 drink menu from Young's Tavern — the Expansion's predecessor — a reminder from finer days when a beer set you back twenty cents and the Bronx was a better drink than a Manhattan. Those prices are gone, but the Expansion still honors those delightfully low drink prices of yesteryear. Artifacts of alcoholism's past live on here too, with antique pinball machines (Show Boat and the more frequently found Triple Play), a couple of shopworn cash registers, and decades' worth of dust and tears lingering in the corners, if you care to look. Sharing the bottle racks are old model cars, and a few toy train sets hold lonely vigils on shelves above the bar.

From grizzled graybeards to Irish expats, the bar caters mostly to regulars, but wandering souls and Saturday night spillover from the Castro can add to the mix. If regulars have all the barstools occupied, a handful of cheap Formica tables offer extra room for leisurely inebriation. For those in need of distraction, there are three TV sets and a pool table in back. The jukebox plies the intersection of country and punk, and the crowd offers just enough gritty authenticity to pull it off. You won't find the Expansion winning any best-of awards anytime soon, and thank god for that. It's a little secret that the dive-ophile might just want to keep to him or herself.

Dive rating: ⚫⚫⚫⚫⚫⚫⚫

Lucky 13

Lucky 13

2140 Market St. (at Church St.)
415-487-1313

Muni: F, J, K, L, M, N, 22, 35, 37

Fans of low-grade spirits and cheap American suds may argue that any-place specializing in high-end European and domestic beer doesn't belong among the cadre of well-loved dive bars. They may be right. Still, despite its beer-snob leanings, the Lucky 13 is a damn fine place to tie one on among the tattooed and pierced masses. One of the holy trinity of bike-punk beer joints in the city — alongside the Toronado and Zeitgeist — the Lucky 13 attempts, with some success, to cultivate a divey personality, most notably offering a perennially dirty bathroom and fairly cheap prices.

Dimly lit by candles and black lights illuminating concert posters, the large bar maintains an even keel most nights even if the jukebox is on a feverish punk rock overload. (A word, however, to those seeking calm places for alcoholic introspection: Skip this place on a Friday or Saturday night.) The bar offers split-level seating, so loners and voyeurs can take in the crowd from above. Otherwise, stick to the ground floor, where tons of tables and barstools offer plenty of seating. A busy pool table in the rear and a well-worn Area 51 video game at the door offer distractions of another sort. And, for fans of Danzig, AC/DC, the Stones, Ministry, and the Sex Pistols, the juke's for you.

To get around bar service that can be slow enough to induce delirium tremens, you may want to order two (or three) and head out to the back patio, where dogs and smokers share their barks and yipes. On a decent Indian summer evening, this outdoor area is one of the finest places in town to imbibe. The Lucky 13 also provides a perfect addendum for patrons who may occasionally opt for liquid lunch and/or dinner — complimentary self-service popcorn at the end of the bar.

Dive rating:

The Transfer

Muni: F, J, K, L, M, N, 22, 35, 37

At the intersection of Church and Market, a name like the Transfer can refer to a multitude of things. It may be just the intersection. Or the slip of paper that lets you get off one Muni line and board another. Then there's the pickup scene, the transfer of conversation, ideas and perhaps bodily fluids. Money from one pocket to another. Drugs from seller to buyer. A sober mind becoming a sotted one. Maybe a contact high seeping through the walls of the medical marijuana clinic next door. All of these things are going on at Church and Market, so anything's possible when it comes to names.

In our story, the Transfer is a serious dive, the kind of place just as likely to be packed Wednesday afternoon as Friday night. Its clientele is fitting of a serious dive as well: daytime tipplers, gravel-voiced speed freaks, half-lucid lunatics, street kids dropping in for a game of pool or pinball, mixed in with plenty of regular Joes (and Steves and Toms). It's primarily a gay bar, but you'll find women and straight folks here as well. What you won't find are many of the muscle-bound pretty boys who frequent the establishments closer to Castro Street proper.

There's usually a drink special written up on a mirror next to the bar. Well drinks are cheap and strong, and domestic drafts are $3. The real reason lots of folks come to the Transfer, however, is because the street side of the bar is all one-way windows, so you can look out, but nobody can look in. It's voyeurism, pure and perfected, the place to see and not be seen.

Dive rating:

CHINATOWN/
NORTH BEACH

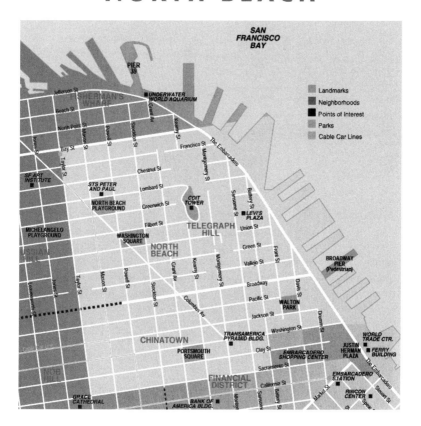

SAN FRANCISCO BAY

	Landmarks
	Neighborhoods
	Points of Interest
	Parks
	Cable Car Lines

PIER 39

Jefferson St

FISHERMAN'S WHARF

UNDERWATER WORLD AQUARIUM

Beach St

North Point St

Bay St

SF ART INSTITUTE

Chestnut St

Francisco St

The Embarcadero

Montgomery St

Taylor St

Powell St

Mason St

Stockton St

Grant Ave

Kearny St

STS PETER AND PAUL

Lombard St

NORTH BEACH PLAYGROUND

Greenwich St

COIT TOWER

Sansome St

Battery St

LEVI'S PLAZA

MICHELANGELO PLAYGROUND

Filbert St

TELEGRAPH HILL

Union St

WASHINGTON SQUARE

NORTH BEACH

Green St

Front St

RUSSIAN HILL

Kearny St

Montgomery St

Vallejo St

BROADWAY PIER (Pedestrian)

Taylor St

Mason St

Powell St

Stockton St

Grant Ave

Columbus Ave

Broadway

Davis St

Pacific St

WALTON PARK

Leavenworth St

Jones St

Jackson St

Drumm St

CHINATOWN

TRANSAMERICA PYRAMID BLDG.

Washington St

WORLD TRADE CTR.

PORTSMOUTH SQUARE

Clay St

EMBARCADERO SHOPPING CENTER

JUSTIN HERMAN PLAZA

FERRY BUILDING

Sacramento St

NOB HILL

FINANCIAL DISTRICT

California St

EMBARCADERO STATION

The Embarcadero

GRACE CATHEDRAL

Montgomery St

Battery St

Sansome St

BANK OF AMERICA BLDG.

RINCON CENTER

Market St

Spear St

Steuart St

Buddha Lounge

901 Grant Ave. (at Washington St.)
415-362-1792

Muni: 1, 15, 30, 45

Wandering Chinatown after dark is one of the quintessential San Francisco experiences, even if you find yourself to be the only person out on these dark and narrow alleyways. With fish and produce markets shuttered and junk shops closed for the night, the streets possess an eerily brilliant silence. However, if an aimless stroll can be something for the soul, a stroll with a purpose can be something else altogether for the liver. Though not as packed with drinking spots as North Beach, Chinatown still offers up its share of divey comforts. One perennial favorite is the Buddha Lounge, a cavernous hole-in-the-wall with a beautiful neon beacon to guide you, sturdy drinks to fill you, and one of the nicest bartenders you're likely to meet.

With bamboo poles supporting a decorative awning above the bar, the Buddha has a feel somewhere in between a modern-day tiki bar and the Chinatown that crumbled in the 1906 earthquake. On the back wall is an enormous painting of the namesake nirvana-seeker, and opposite that wall is an oversize dragon mural. While there's not much room to dance, revelers occasionally bump and grind to the funk-heavy and soul-chocked jukebox. Far friendlier than some of the other bars in the neighborhood, the Buddha does have its regulars, but the bottom line is that the place simply isn't big enough to hold too many people. Folks tend to stop in and move on as the night progresses. If it's too full, you can always drop by on your way back home.

A word of warning though — if the bartender offers to buy you a shot, steer clear of the curiously round ceramic bottle on the top shelf. The truly adventurous soul may find Ng Ka Py the perfect excuse to let one's liver live dangerously, but be advised that this herbal-flavored plum wine will stick with you (and to you) for the rest of the night. On one plum-scented evening, my drinking buddy Krumpledump was unable to drink or eat or even talk until he had a chance to walk off the remnants of his encounter with this potent brew.

Dive rating: ⬤ ⬤ ⬤ ⬤ ⬤ ⬤

Columbus Café

562 Green St. (at Columbus Ave.)
415-291-0818

Muni: 15, 30, 41, 39, 45

It may not be too pleasing on the eyes upon first (and second and third) glance, but the Columbus Café will definitely please the leather in your pocket or purse — two-for-one beers from 4 p.m. to 8 p.m. daily. For those who can't go out until after the vampires have risen, you can still get a pint of Pilsner Urquell for $1 anytime (except Friday and Saturday nights), which is a fine way to live upscale at a dive-licious price.

While it can get busy at happy hour with the after-work crowd and is often overrun with prime-time tipplers, you should find the Columbus a bit emptier than some of its North Beach neighbors after the midnight hour. You'll also find that there's a downstairs lounge (horrendously named the Voodoo Room, as of this writing) on weekends for chilling, playing pool, and smoking, legally. Up in the main bar, you can thank those beautiful minds behind beer marketing for the appealing scenery — neon beer signs and Corona surfboards constitute the primary mood-setters.

On weekends, couples and hopeful singles flock to the bar to see and be seen, play pool, and indulge in that favorite of North Beach traditions: making a drunken fool of oneself. While it's not a day-and-night sports bar, you can expect a big turnout and lots of hollering on game days. One touch you won't find at your average dive is an enormous flat-screen TV for grotesquely proper sports viewing.

Dive rating:

Crow Bar

401 Broadway St. (at Montgomery St.)
415-488-2769

Muni: 12, 15, 41

Nestled among the city's most neon-loaded, tourist-packed stretch of strip club hell is a tiny slice of divey peace called the Crow Bar. Though it has its own crunch of after-work swillers stopping in for happy hour, it's one of the few places in North Beach where you can drop in at 11 p.m. on a Saturday night and still get a seat or a slot at one of the two pool tables.

The cavernous place has exposed brick on one wall and some tasteful black and whites on another. Avian-themed cornball décor peeks out here and there, and a "Why lie, it's for beer" cardboard sign next to the TV is a nice street-level touch. And, if you've ever wondered why there are so few $2 bills in the world, it's because they've all been tacked up behind the bar here. Fancy beer flows by the pint — a fair deal at $3.50 — and the juke-box is one of the city's best, loaded with the Supersuckers, Me First and the Gimme Gimmes, Slayer, Ween, Morphine, and many, many standards of the punk/rockabilly canon.

During happy hour, expect tame, it's-still-light-out fun, such as the time when a group of coworkers and I plied our boss with shots and beer until he was doing push-ups and dancing around the bar. Later in the night, you can expect more garden-variety bar excitement. One friend of a friend got in a pissing match over his spot on the pool list and ended up tossing his beer in somebody's face and getting shithoused and bounced out into the night. Such episodes are rare, but this is prime North Beach real estate, and well, let's face it, your chance of running into a drunken asshole on Broadway is worth putting money on. My buddy Greg says he frequently runs into off-work strippers in here, which is probably true since you can't walk twenty paces down the street without getting a personal invite to see the best show on earth. But most of the times I've come to the Crow Bar, it's all guys.

Dive rating: ● ● ● ●

Grant & Green

There's only one reason to go to the Grant & Green — because shakin' your ass is a great way to get a piece of ass. The formula is fairly straight-forward: A largely monochromatic crowd comes together around cheap drinks and cheaper music, as there's never a cover, and always live music. Don't expect the next up-and-coming indie techno whatevero thing — think more poor man's Rolling Stones. Patrons range from middle-aged and desperate to young and gorgeous. If you're willing to prove yourself on the dance floor, you'll have a much better chance of finding your way home in fair company. On busy weekend nights, things get a little too bumpy and grindy as drunken groups of North Beach bar crawlers descend for a chance to get down to the white boy shuffle.

Dedicated cheap-asses will be happy to find Pabst in the bottle, and those with fancier tastes have a decent selection of beer and top-shelf booze.

The actions peaks at about 1 a.m., as patrons drift out in groups of two and three to the corner in front of the bar. Those with unrequited cravings of the gastronomical sort can satisfy their hunger across the street at Golden Boy Pizza, a North Beach institution where you'll never come up empty unless your wallet is.

Dive rating:

Grassland

Grassland

905 Kearny St. (at Jackson St.)
415-362-9570

Muni: 1, 12, 15, 41

For eons, hungry patrons waiting in line outside the Chinatown staple House of Nanking have pondered the meaning of the curious line, "Where good friends and girls meet" above Grassland's door. Those who have wandered by looking for either girls or good friends have been similarly confused. One friend swears a friend of a friend told him it was a place where one might find a lady for certain pleasures, if one were inclined to buy more than drinks — and it's an easy legend to believe, as Grassland is sandwiched among a number of massage parlors along Kearny Street. Professional bar legend collector Boris says his sources tell him this is a place where pretty girls working in connection with the bartender will shake you down for drinks, which when served, are watered down so that said girls can soberly continue to shake you down on your spiral toward drunkenness.

As colorful and seedy as that all sounds, on any night I've ever stopped in, I've been one of only a few patrons, if not the only drinker, with no ladies of the night, no drink-shaking bar ladies, no ladies at all, in sight.

Within a thong's width of many of North Beach's packed and obnoxious bars, Grassland nonetheless never seems to fill up, and will only occasionally draw in a few lost tourists for a quick round. There's plenty to look at, but it's probably not the place to go looking for lively conversation, or conversation at all. With the chili pepper-shaped Christmas lights turned off, the place is a dark and silent hole punctuated by occasional outbursts from solitary drunks and the clinking of one of the two Triple Play machines.

A buzz can be well spent trying to decipher the mysterious scribblings left in Sharpie ink on the loads of $1 bills from years past that are tacked up on the bar for posterity. Drinks won't cost you more than a few of those dollars' contemporary companions. Curious tastes for snacks or cigarettes can be answered here: In addition to cough drops, hungry bar-goers will find unusual offerings such as squid chips. And, smokers ought to check out the Yun Yan or 555 brand cigarettes on sale behind the bar, just to see what they're smoking in the old country.

Dive rating:

Hawaii West

729 Vallejo St. (at Stockton St.)
415-362-3220

Muni: 12, 15, 30, 41, 45

Only minutes from the garish neon of some of the most overdecorated bars in the city is a place with painted Styrofoam seashells embedded in the wall, and card tables and folding chairs by way of seating arrangements. If there were a breeze here, you'd hear the rustling of long-dead palm fronds overhead. If there were a tropical monsoon, you could take cover beneath the sheet metal roof over the bar — the rain gutters are an especially nice touch. A friend who knows the ins and outs of such things said there's more to Hawaii West than meets the eye. I'm not sure what that means, but I do know that I like what I see at any rate.

The only tiki bar in North Beach, Hawaii West has a fabulous feel to it, whether or not you are a fan of such schlocky décor. (I am.) Though it's just a block off the main strip, it's usually empty, even on Saturday night. In the back of the bar is "Hawaii West Café" — not that I've seen it up and running during my few visits — offering island specialties such as dogs, chicken, and "ribbs." Behind the bar is probably the kindest bartender I've come across in San Francisco. There's Sinatra on the jukebox and a barely crooked pool table where you can usually get a cue in. And if you want to take a piece of the island home with you, buy a lei at the bar for a five-spot. Don't worry, the flowers won't wilt before you get home. Plastic flowers never do.

Dive rating: ●●●●●●●

The Hungry I

546 Broadway St. (at Columbus Ave.)
415-362-7763

Muni: 12, 15, 30, 41, 45

This place — through combination of name, location, and changing identity — has had its sticky fingers in every phase of North Beach history. Decades ago, the Hungry I, then located on Jackson Street, was a cutting-edge performance space where folks like Richard Pryor, Jonathan Winters, and Lenny Bruce wowed crowds. (Bruce's infamous obscenity trial arose out of one of his Hungry I performances.) For years, it was one of San Francisco's defining avant-garde nightspots. Mort Sahl, Vince Guaraldi, the Kingston Trio and others all recorded gigs there. Years later, the Hungry I relocated to Broadway and redefined itself as a strip club. And while schooled aficionados of such entertainment may debate the merits of one club over another, discussing the wonders of silicone, hair extensions, and tattoos, I'll stick to subjects I know. And what I know is that, unlike in most of the strip clubs in this city, you can get a drink at the Hungry I — due to the fact that the ladies only go topless rather than parading around full frontal and back.

Fans of SF classics will remember the interior from Dirty Harry and a handful of other locally filmed TV shows and movies. Those who pay a visit will also notice an antique oak bar that, according to one knowledgeable North Beach historian (also a DJ at a neighboring strip club), dates back 150 years to Barbary Coast days. According to local legend, this particular bar was apparently a chowder house in a very distant former life. This place breathes history, though whether or not you can smell it over the stench of sweaty cash is another question entirely. Fans of other obscure historical tidbits may relish the rumor that Courtney Love once straddled a pole here.

Bear in mind that between the $5 to $10 cover charge, the $7 drinks, and the girls constantly shaking you down for tips, drinks, or lap dances, this ain't a place where cheap-asses go to get their rocks off. If you come here with money in your pocket, don't expect to leave with any. That said, if you can time your drinking just right, you can take advantage of $4 drink specials every hour or so — and the mind-numbing (a quick path to your wallet) strength of these cocktails means that you're actually getting your money's worth, if you have any money or worth left after a few.

Dive rating:

Kennedy's

Kennedy's

1040 Columbus Ave. (at Chestnut St.)
415-441-8855

Muni: 30; Powell-Mason cable car

Not really a dive, but a curiosity nonetheless, Kennedy's seems to thrive on unlikely combinations. It's an Irish pub without much of an Irish personality (old maritimey worm-eaten beams and the shrine to Jerry Garcia kind of throw off the effect). It's an indoor space — with an Indian curry restaurant occupying a pretty large section. It's an outdoor space — with a wonderful view of the recently demolished projects. It can be fairly mellow — and overflowing on weekends. And, the crowd is a 50-50 split between typical North Beach Banana Republicans and cute young hippie-types.

One thing, however, unifies all the disparate elements — an abundance of beer. The main attractions are the unbeatable $2 pints of Guinness and Beamish at all hours, and the Pabst pitchers at the very divey rate of $5. Suds lovers will find a couple dozen micros on tap, with another hundred or so in the bottle. It's the alcoholic's ego boost, a logbook where die-hard drinkers catalogue their attempts to drink 100 different brews.

Grizzled old-timers steer clear of this place, so if that's who you want to spend your time with, make a note to steer clear yourself. But Kennedy's is a fab place to drink on the cheap, whether you are a tourist stuck in a Fisherman's Wharf hotel, are getting warmed up for a show at Bimbo's across the street, or just want to try something off the well-worn North Beach path. The bartenders are first-rate, and the patrons talk a good game. All in all, it's a bar with a uniquely strange, but strangely welcoming vibe.

Dive rating:

La Rocca's Corner

957 Columbus Ave. (at Chestnut St.)
415-674-1266

Muni: 30; Powell-Mason cable car

A small, pie-shaped slice of drinking bliss in one of the more heavily guide-booked parts of the city, La Rocca's bills itself as the bar "Where Tourists Meet the Locals." While I've never met any tourists here, the locals are quite a presence. Steadily inhabited by a coterie of hard-drinking, loud-laughing, dice-smacking fellas, La Rocca's is a place where the shit-talk flies, sports banter rarely stops, and women are sometimes as sparse as North Beach parking spots.

With cable cars rattling just outside the enormous windows and lots of framed, local black and whites slapped on the wall, the place can seem, well, a little too San Francisco-themed for those who prefer drab environs in which to sink into a stupor. But the astute observer will notice a few choice gems of the city's finest moments on the walls: neighborhood son Joe DiMaggio in his Yankees stripes (hiss . . .), the Niners crushing the Bengals in Super Bowl 16, and a signed poster of gun-toting heiress Patty Hearst as Tania, SLA warrior. Local lore has it that La Rocca's was a Mafia hangout in one of its past lives, but I'm wondering why they'd pick a place with so many windows.

If you're hoping to save a few bucks, order a drink special (the $5 Pabst-Smir comes to mind — a PBR draft and "cosmo shot" of Smirnoff, whatever that is). Otherwise, the drinks are steeper than your average dive — drafts are $4, name drinks $5. With Bimbo's just a few doors down, the place can get a bit crowded with hipsters aiming to pre-lubricate before the show.

While the drinks are overpriced and the regulars a tough crowd to break in with, there's still something charming about La Rocca's. It might just be that it's one of those places where you get a glimpse at a part of the city most people never see. Or it could be that the Mexican place next door will deliver your nachos to your barstool. Either way, La Rocca's neon motto, "This is it!" somehow rings true, whatever it is.

Dive rating: ●●●●●

Li Po

Tucked away from the hustle of Grant Avenue's arched rooftops beneath a Chinese-style lantern, the terminally empty Li Po is an ode to Chinatown isolation, as well as a cozy place to get lit up before meandering on toward North Beach's numerous swilleries. Not that you have much of a chance of going anywhere besides lushville once you slide into one of the sticky red Naugahyde booths in the back. Drinks are reasonably priced, and far more importantly, strong enough to make Li Po a requisite stop after any questionable Chinatown meal. Slightly strange dim sum? Curiously tingly feelings after Chairman Mao's Fried Chicken? Not to worry, Li Po's got an ancient Eastern remedy and it's called cheap alcohol. Dedicated Bud drinkers here feel the call of the Orient and trade in one kind of lowbrow suds for another, finding Tsingtao to be the stronger but not much tastier Chinese equivalent to Anheuser-Busch's reigning champ.

Decor ranges from colorful Chinese New Year decoration leftovers (not so colorful a decade or two after the celebration) to epic murals whose epic has long since faded. A gilded Buddha altar presides serenely (if a bit dustily) over the corner behind the bar. Old-school vidiots will appreciate the sit-down Ms. Pac-Man just inside the entry.

While the clientele can include a table of lost tourists or curious locals, more often than not you'll find Li Po near-empty on prime dive nights (Sun.–Wed.). Older Chinese guys sometimes wander in on slow nights to make small talk with the bartender. Beyond that, it's you and a barkeep who'd rather pour you another strong one than make weak conversation.

Dive rating:

Mr. Bing's

Mr. Bing's

201 Columbus Ave. (at Pacific Ave.)
415-362-1545

Muni: 12, 15, 41

Curiosity draws some into this triangular building with its unusual V-shaped bar and panel of windows looking out onto a busy stretch of Columbus. But once inside, there's little to keep you here other than the strong, cheap drinks and a bartender who will let you indulge yourself in whatever trouble said cheap, strong drinks might get you into. On one particular visit, a pair of Irishmen drunkenly belted Tom Jones tunes for half an hour before the bartender rather meekly (and unsuccessfully) tried to 86 them from the joint. Try your luck. You can probably get away with worse.

Don't come here looking to pick up on your next quick thing, unless your particular pleasure comes in the package of elderly Chinese men drinking solo. Also, you might just want to bring friends or maintain your own internal monologue, as talk can be short on some nights. Mostly, Mr. Bing's is the kind of place you always wondered about, stopped in for a couple strong ones, and then stopped wondering about. Even so, some Chinatown/North Beach frequent fliers swear by the place and make the cheap Naugahyde stools at the Formica bar top a requisite stop on any evening's alcoholic ambulation.

Attentive drinkers will notice a dozen pool trophies on a high shelf above the bar despite the lack of a pool table. Competitive-minded folks may need to satisfy their urges at that bastion of video golf bliss, Golden Tee. You also may be able to get in on a friendly game of chance with some of Mr. Bing's regulars, where a firm command of Mandarin or Cantonese is likely to come in handy.

Dive rating:

Red's Place

672 Jackson St. (at Grant Ave.)
415-956-4490

Muni: 1, 12, 15, 30, 45

Chinatown's oldest bar is a dyed-in-the-wool dive, seemingly always boasting at least one sleeping patron, mirrors coated with six decades of smoke, and drinks as cheap as you're likely to find in the neighborhood. While its low-key customer base rarely pulls in lost travelers from nearby and better-known spots like Li Po or the Buddha Lounge, it's nonetheless worth a visit, if only to get a taste of grit and authenticity in a part of town long on caricature and stereotype.

The bar has a certain amount of class despite its unkempt appearance. Lots of said mirrors, subdued decorative elements of the Orient, and bright lighting try to make the place sparkle, if a place can sparkle under a layer or two of dust. The juke in front doesn't get much play, and a busted jukebox is crammed in a corner next to the homemade bar extension at the back of the place. Most patrons tune into one of the two TVs — one usually blasting a Chinese soap opera, the other offering soundless Westerns or other fluff. A place you'd never expect those infernal video trivia machines to penetrate, but alas, even here, one can interact with bad computer games for money all night, if one is so inclined. The rest of the crowd generally keeps it mellow. Still, there's something really appealing about the place. If it weren't so terminally dead most nights, you might want to move in here. Just bring a dust rag and a can of Pledge.

Dive rating: ●●●●●●●●●

Red's Place

Spec's

Spec's

12 Saroyan Pl. (off Columbus Ave. near Broadway St.)
415-421-4112

Muni: 12, 15, 41

Vaguely maritime in its approach, Spec's is one part curio shop for every two parts bar. Solo drinkers will find an evening's amusement in the literally hundreds of dust-laden and historic items tacked to every square inch of wall and ceiling real estate: old flags, shark jaws, shrunken heads, model ships, wartime photos, Native American wood sculptures, an enormous painted tortoise shell, etc. Ever wondered how big a walrus penis is? Take a look above the bar. Spec's is also home to some of the best bumper stickers you've never seen on the highway: Stop Solar Energy; Mutants for Nuclear Power; Village Idiots for a Toxic Environment; Ask me about my vow of silence, etc.

Those with hopes of finding any alcoholic remnants of Beat-era San Francisco might just stumble across something poetic here — if it can't be found in the bottom of a glass. While the crowd can veer toward the youngish and well-heeled, you can still find goatee-sporting, blazer-wearing grayheads who shuck and jive Beat-style with the bartenders and fellow oldsters. The staff tends toward the artist/intellectual-type, putting Spec's on a different plane from most of its neighborhood contemporaries.

Though there are plenty of stools at the long wooden bar, most people arrive in groups and gather around tables to talk among themselves. But with the slightly upper-scale Tosca next door and close proximity to a number of other bars, Spec's and its resident alleyway offer plenty of opportunities to meet people, bum smokes or a puff of something more intoxicating, and find new friends at least for an evening.

Dive rating: ●●●●●

Vieni Vieni Lucky Spot

1431 Stockton St. (at Vallejo St.)
415-391-7633

Muni: 12, 15, 30, 41, 45

If there's one rule to dives, it's that if somebody gets shot, the joint is a dive. Vieni Vieni qualified for that revered honor long before a patron gave a bartender a special 2 a.m. tip a few years back, but that incident certainly sealed the deal. Last call, apparently, for more than alcohol.

Don't be deterred though. This Italian-cum-Chinese watering hole is in reality far from being a murderer's row. Still, there's a gritty authenticity about this place that defies explanation. Duck your head out the back door to an alley that squad cars fly down from time to time, and you'll feel like you're in a Chinatown you've never seen. Maybe it's the trio of middle-aged Chinese guys discussing their relationship woes. Or maybe it's the drunken lady passed out on the bar for a couple hours. Anywhere else, a bartender would 86 her. But then again, you can't be too cautious with the regulars.

The jukebox is stacked with jazz classics from decades back — their tracks permanently attached to the wall above; "new" stuff still rotates through about once a decade (latest release circa 1988). More frequently, a pall of silence hangs in the hazy air as muted conversation wanders between broken English and busted drunk. Old-school vidiots can revisit lost Saturdays of years past at the sit-down Ms. Pac-Man and Arkanoid along the wall, and short-armed sharks can get their game on at the undersized pool table in the back. The patrons — a mix of ordinary neighborhood folks, old Italian sailor types, and middle-aged Chinese men — generally don't care for any of these highfalutin games. Sometimes the crack of dice rattles the room, but more often than not, it's either quiet talk or inner voices.

Dive rating: ●●●●●●●●

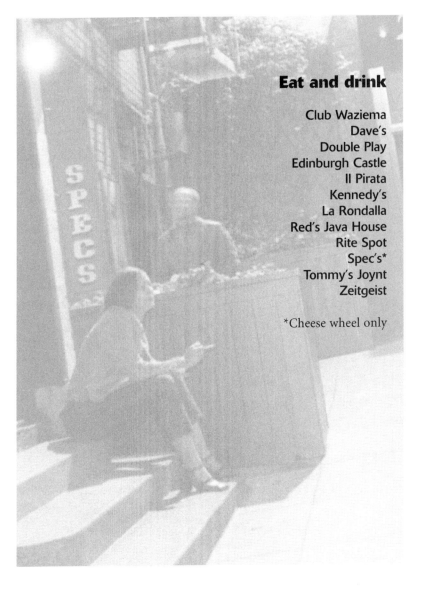

Eat and drink

Club Waziema
Dave's
Double Play
Edinburgh Castle
Il Pirata
Kennedy's
La Rondalla
Red's Java House
Rite Spot
Spec's*
Tommy's Joynt
Zeitgeist

*Cheese wheel only

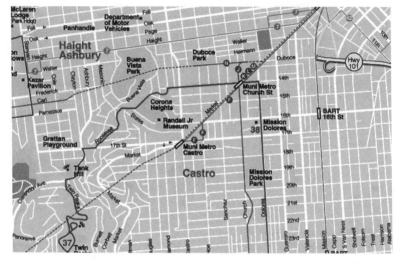

Haight

HAIGHT/
WESTERN ADDITION

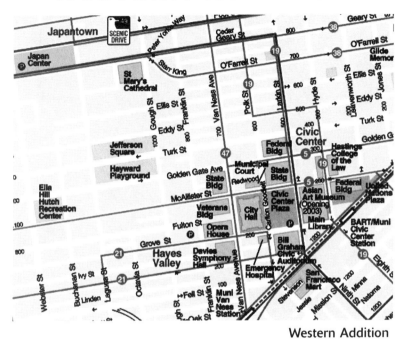

Western Addition

Chances

298 Divisadero St. (at Page St.)
415-255-6101

Muni: 6, 7, 24, 66, 71

A busy neighborhood dive offering pool and plenty of table space, Chances isn't going to win any prizes for decoration or ambiance, and we can thank the bar gods for that. (No red candles or local artists' work here.) The young clientele is drawn mostly from the immediate neighborhood, as this isn't the kind of place you'd cross town to visit. But it *is* the kind of place you wouldn't mind finding yourself in after spending an hour or two waiting to be served at one of Lower Haight's busier hipster draws or wandering all of Divisadero looking for a whisky sour.

Good-natured shit-talking around the two pool tables is a near constant, so if you didn't come here with friends, you might leave having made a few. Single and single-minded folks may find Chances the ideal place to arrange a future date — either for when your drink's finished or for the rest of your life. Even those with kindergarten-level conversation skills will find the bartenders a talkative bunch as they fish for on-the-clock excitement and tips.

Prices may not please penny-pinchers, but rest assured that your dollars won't be ill spent. The pour tends toward the generous, and unlike many of the beer-and-wine-only bars along Divisadero, you can get a *real* drink at Chances. The jukebox is well stocked with staples — Pixies, Hendrix, Bowie, Elton, the Stones, the usual — offering yet another chance to work on the soundtrack to your life.

Dive rating:

SAN FRANCISCO'S BEST DIVE BARS

Club Waziema

543 Divisadero St. (at Hayes St.)
415-346-6641

Muni: 21, 24

Those who rarely have the chops to close the bar will find a night at Club Waziema an ego-boosting event. Ostensibly open until midnight, this quiet and rarely crowded Ethiopian hole-in-the-wall often closes at 11 p.m. or earlier, especially if all the early-to-bed locals have dropped off after their timid night's revelries.

A magnet for the city's small community of Ethiopian expats, Waziema offers a dozen beers on tap, just as many bottles, and a couple varieties of bar-quality wine, which almost make up for the lack of hard liquor. Adventurous eaters can try Ethiopian cuisine while they drink, matching their meal with honey wine or Ethiopian beer.

The velvety Victorian wallpaper is an incongruous match, with huge palm fans hung on the wall, and Bass and Guinness lights offer strange competition for a mock-old Budweiser sign. In the back room, mediocre pool players trade shots surrounded by the work of local artists. The jukebox offers a solid and imaginative mix of old funk, soul, and rock, but I much preferred the owner's stacks of Afropop and other current-day African artists. Old-world charm also occasionally wanders in off the street, as nighttime hawkers offer everything from steering wheel covers to underground hip-hop cassettes.

While it's a low-key place to begin a night, especially if you wish to have a little pleasant chitchat with your fellow bar-hoppers, those seeking strong drinks, lunatic conversation and hours beyond what your grandmother would enjoy should imbibe elsewhere.

Dive rating: ●●●●●

Finnegan's Wake

937 Cole St. (at Carl St.)
415-731-6779

Muni: N, 6, 37, 43

Finnegan's Wake is the closest thing to a dive in a part of town where city kids want to live after they've decided to grow up. A Cole Valley staple for more than twenty-five years, the place doesn't offer much for lovers of Pabst, Busch, or Oly, but there are more than a dozen beers on tap at fair prices and specials on shots and drinks that'll warm the wallet of any budget-conscious swiller.

With its cozy wood paneling, Elvis detritus behind the bar, and quirky signage ("Shoplifters will be violated"), Finnegan's has cultivated a comfortable local vibe. During the day, it is filled with mellow regulars, and at night, a younger crowd beautifies things a bit. However, no matter whether it's day or night, the music never seems too loud, the wait for a drink never too long, and the patrons never too out of control (except after exam days at nearby UCSF when med students sometimes indulge in a little post-cram bingeing).

Those who prefer distraction to conversation can while their time away at the pool table, darts, or pinball. On those rare days when it's actually warm, folks head to the patio out back, where a couple of tables in the open air make a decent smoking parlor. Even so, the inside of the bar is still large enough that even on busy nights, there seems to always be an empty corner to call home. Curious drinkers have long wondered about the room upstairs, where a mystery bar that no one seems to ever drink at captivates the imagination of those who pine for bars of their very own.

Perhaps in deference to its crew of stodgy old-timers — or simply to rein in the excesses of the next generation of drinkers — Finnegan's also enforces one Luddite rule rarely seen in our hi-tech wonderland: a ban on mobile phones. Turn it off before you tilt them back.

Dive rating:

Fulton Street

1785 Fulton St. (at Masonic Ave.)
415-292-7564

Muni: 5, 43

An immense two-story bar favored by beer-guzzling USF students, Fulton Street is a wonderful dive if you happen to catch it on study night. The downstairs features a dozen booths, two pool tables, a punk-loaded jukebox, and joy of anachronistic joys, an old-fashioned cigarette machine tucked away beneath the stairway (although $6 a pack ain't exactly old-fashioned). Upstairs is more of the same: brown carpet bearing Jackson Pollackesque stains, another pool table, and a second bar so that lazy drinkers don't have to navigate the stairs in order to refuel.

While the tap selection and drink specials veer toward those favored by college students with a few extra bucks to spend, you'll still find strong well drinks and PBR in the bottle. Prices are fair, and in this bar-deprived neighborhood, you could do worse, like stopping into the mysterious Café Daebul a few doors down, where you'll be charged $7 for a drink. Farther on down the street is jazzclub-cum-nightclub Storyville, which also adds a few castaways to the Fulton Street mix.

When Fulton Street opened a few years back, it filled a sorely needed void in the neighborhood. And because few places have opened in the meantime, it remains an immensely popular, frequently packed neighborhood institution, with close proximity to a university. While this means you'll find competition at the pool table from peachfuzz-sporting youngsters, you can still pretend you're a kid at the head-to-head driving video game, alien shoot-'em-up Area 51, or the photo booth. A sister spot to North Beach's Crow Bar, Fulton Street offers the same low-key vibe in a neighborhood where you can actually find a parking spot.

Dive rating: ●●●●●

The Gold Cane

1569 Haight St. (at Clayton St.)
415-626-1112

Muni: 7, 33, 37, 43, 66, 71

Not likely to win an award for anything other than the enormous moose head staring down the front door, the Gold Cane is what you would see in the dictionary under the definition of "nondescript." With cheap tables, cheap barstools, and décor that barely breathes, the Gold Cane has as much character as a Subway sandwich shop. This is the place you want to be after the breakup fight, as the faux stained glass behind the bar, faux Tiffany lamps, and multitude of TV screens are unlikely to offer too much distraction from your obligatory misery. That said, it's also the perfect place to bring a prospective partner to see if his/her personality is enough to keep you interested, as the bar won't.

Voyeurs can keep an eye on sidewalk strollers from the tinted window facing the street, but most patrons come to drink a few and watch the game. A handful of beers on tap, plus cheap fares on the liquor train, makes this a decent place to start out a night, or hide out from the Haight Street shuffle.

Fifty-year-old photos on the back wall show off local history, but the present is long gone from this place. A fairly tame jukebox offers little competition with conversation. If you're looking for action or intrigue, head elsewhere. However, if you've got sorrows to wallow in or are alone on game day, the Cane is the perfect place to not stand out.

Dive rating:

The Gold Cane

John Murio's Trophy Room 1811 Haight St. (at Shrader St.)
415-752-2971

Muni: 7, 33, 37, 43, 66, 71

Dating back to before the neighborhood's famous Summer of Love era made it a hit with hippies, then hipsters and now tourists, Murio's was open in 1960, when former athlete John Murio decided he needed a place to show off all his trophies (hence the name of the bar). Many of those shining homages to Murio's exploits are sadly gone, their cases now home to dusty Day of the Dead figurines. As a consolation, in the back near the pool tables, the bar's numerous sharks have claimed wall space for their even more numerous plaques and awards from pool tournaments.

Drinks are cheap as shit, but occasionally poured that way too. Let your bartender know if he stiffs you with a limp one. Beer comes from a small army of taps, and the bottle selection is solid enough to keep brand-snobs happy enough. The odd mish-mosh décor (old beer lights, obligatory deer head with American flag bandanna, etc.) is an eclectically satisfying match for the punk-heavy but nonetheless wide-ranging jukebox: NOFX, the Faces, Dead Boys, Pixies, Devo, Aretha, assorted 1980s detritus, and even the only-on-Haight compilation "Conversion Van Classics."

Patrons are a mix of jaded neighborhood ex-punks, the odd curious tourist, and overwhelmed shoppers from Amoeba Records' mammoth aisles. If you don't bring any friends along, don't expect to make any, but you'll find the clientele civil enough to not steal your drink if you head to the can. While the aroma of spilled beer may seem a century old, those with a nose for a true dive recognize that's the smell of heaven, where fate is a barstool and the angelic choir sings in a chorus of clinked glasses.

Dive rating: ●●●●●●●●

John Murio's Trophy Room

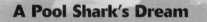

A Pool Shark's Dream

The Brown Jug
Cassidy's
Edinburgh Castle
El Amigo
Grandma's
John Murio's Trophy Room
Kilowatt
Route 101
Sadie's Flying Elephant
Wild Side West

Molotov's

On a recent visit, Molotov's appeared to have undergone a major transformation. Banished were the overpowering aromas of piss, vomit, and yesterday's beer, which for many years had been the bar's trademark. Did this signal a new mop bucket in the closet, or a brave new philosophy of cleanliness? Was the new aluminum covering on the pillars and support beams part of the upgrade for the Lower Haight's edgiest dive? Was the bartender about to offer me a smile and ask what I wanted, sir? Fortunately, the answer to all these questions was a resounding *no*, as Molotov's retains much of its original, tainted aura, even with the few aesthetic and sanitary improvements.

Back when the neighborhood was actually defined by its tattoo-wearing, multiply pierced, green-haired punk denizens making a life for themselves on the edge of the ghetto, the Midtown was a gathering spot for such locals. Over time, the Lower Haight lost much of its ragged glory and Midtown closed and morphed into Molotov's — a story whose sordid details I've heard enough times to have forgotten them all. While it's a pale shade of its former self, Molotov's is still a dark and dingy place where you can order a stiff one along a drinking strip dominated by beer bars.

Folks here range from slumming hipster types to aging punks to genuinely sketchy neighborhood freaks — a fairly palatable mix. If the jukebox is a punk pleasuredome, the pool table is a hustler's dream. The folks here know their game and don't appreciate unpracticed players wasting valuable stick time. Despite the rugged-seeming character on display any given night here, the crowd is actually a friendly bunch, for the most part. Even the cursing, surly bartenders only half mean it, half the time.

Dive rating: ●●●●●●●

Peacock Lounge

552 Haight St. (at Steiner St.)
415-621-9850

Muni: 6, 7, 22, 66, 71

The Peacock Lounge does exist, but there is a better than average chance that you'll never actually see it. You see, the Peacock is generally open to the public only when someone has rented out the space. That's called a private party, you say. Well, maybe, but a "private" party at the Peacock usually means that the general public is welcome. Strange? Yes, but why question these little mysteries of life? Just remember that when the doors are open, come on in, buy a drink, and play everyone's favorite drinking game, "Whose party is this?"

True to its moniker, the Peacock's walls are hung with psychedelic 1970s impressions of its namesake bird, dimly lit by ailing strands of Christmas lights. A dingy, oft-soaked carpet holds odorific testament to years of infrequent parties and drunken revelers, not to mention the sorry state of the lounge's power vacuum. The front room is small and frequently packed, overflowing into a much larger back room with tables and a dance floor. On the way to the ladies' restroom, a full-service kitchen awaits a cook who's never been seen.

Behind the bar, marbleized mirrors and aluminum foil-lined bottle racks display a lean but serviceable selection of booze. Beer drinkers choose between what's on hand — usually Bud, Sierra, and Heineken — and what's cold, as there are no coolers here, just one hardworking barkeep, her grandfatherly barback, and dozens of bags of ice. Those with rigid dive definitions may want to abandon them at the door. Shots and mixed drinks are $5 apiece here, and they're poured to the milliliter. Beers are $3 and $4. It's perhaps best to arrive here with your buzz already intact, as fighting your way to the lone bartender, as well as the stiff price of keeping abreast of your alcoholism, can make this a tough place to begin an evening (if you even knew that you were going to begin your evening here in the first place).

Dive rating: ●●●●●●●

Trax

1437 Haight St. (at Ashbury St.)
415-864-4213

Muni: 6, 7, 33, 37, 43, 66, 71

Hoping to transform itself into something better, this boxcar of a bar recently underwent an unfortunate facelift that fortunately couldn't eviscerate its diviness. In an effort to make this tiny hole appear larger, mirrors now grace the bar's two long walls, sending sotted tipplers into Matrix-like spasms. This, along with neo-deco accoutrements, the deep red bar top, and experimental bottle racks, may get your head spinning trying to figure out the decorative strategy. But don't despair; underneath the cleaner and hip-looking enhancements, this is still the same old friendly neighborhood gay bar it's always been.

Tuesday is the night to be here — $2 beers. But on pretty much any given night the bar offers an excuse to get intoxicated on the cheap: Will & Grace night drink specials, 49er game day specials, etc. Drinkers in need of a serious hangover are encouraged to try whatever might pour from the twin frozen drink tanks: hurricanes, margaritas, Kahlua drinks, and other concoctions that arrive with all the ceremony of a 7-11 Slurpee. Regular prices aren't bottom-barrel cheap, but they're fair enough to keep you from losing your stupor.

A-gays and pickup fellers have left Trax to a mellower crowd of less beautiful, but far friendlier creatures. While the bar does draw primarily a gay crowd, hetero couples and others also stop in for games on the lone pool table or for straight talk at a nice price. Some of the city's friendliest bartenders can be found here, and the owners may in fact be the bar's biggest regulars. All in all, it's as unpretentious as they come, and, despite its best intentions, still remains a divey place to spend an evening.

Dive rating:

THE MISSION/
BERNAL HEIGHTS

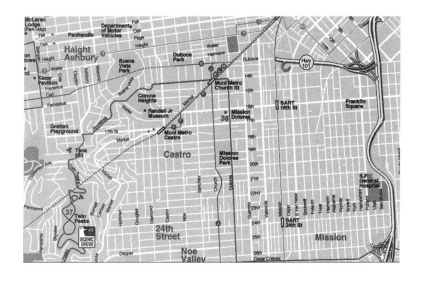

500 Club

500 Club

The fabulously colorful neon marquee has been a beacon for dive-seekers for years, even if the 500 Club's glory days of true divehood are long gone. Yes, you'll still find Pabst Blue Ribbon on tap, but damn, paying $3 for a pint is an insult to any connoisseur of quality cheap beer. Fancier suds will set you back $4 a pint, and name drinks will cost you a Lincoln. Discount drinkin', this ain't. Even so, the gorgeous wood paneling and overabundance of beer-brand mirrors on the walls recall finer days and cheaper buzzes.

While the clientele has shifted toward the well-heeled and homogenous of late, you'll still find the occasional old-school Mission soul angling for nods beneath a funny boho hat. Most people arrive in groups, packing themselves into one of the gorgeous booths in the main room. The pool room serves as the overflow area on crowded nights, but it doesn't have quite the same feel as the main room. But it doesn't matter where you sit, stand, or salivate on a game day when the place turns into a veritable sports bar, with popcorn, wieners, and all.

Those who like to enjoy bars the way they ought to be (meaning without a lot of rich fuckheads giving the place another incentive to raise drink prices) ought to patronize the 500 Club on a slow, rainy weeknight, when the drink specials are on and the jukebox is all yours. With Tom Waits, the Beasties, Bo Diddley, trashy '80s rock, and a handful of surprises, it has long been one of the city's finest.

Another bonus: Morning drinkers take note — the 500 Club opens at 6 a.m. on weekends.

Dive rating:

3300 Club

3300 Mission St. (at 29th St.)
415-826-6886

Muni: J, 14, 24, 26, 49, 67

While the neighborhood's Irish foundation has been swept beneath a wave of Latino immigration, only to be followed by new waves of gentrifying hordes, this outer Mission — or if you subscribe to catchy attempts to redefine neighborhoods, Deep Mission — corner bar is a throwback to an earlier era when men were men and having a drink with some friends was a lifetime's vocation. From a photo on one side of the bar, it's clear the place has some history. The building itself dates back to before the 1906 quake, but it's made several transformations — both physical and philosophical — in the intervening decades. Good news to history buffs: A bar has occupied the place continuously since 1933. In a town on constant reinvention, this is one place where you can clink glasses with the ghosts of drinkers past.

Once the hangout of union members and longshoremen, the 3300 Club has adjusted to its changing environs little by little. Though one is still likely to hear the lilt of an Irish accent or two in the place — not to mention the Pogues, U2, and other Celtic rockers — you'll hear plenty of Spanish spoken here. Frequented by a stable of older couples and solitary drinkers, the 33 also attracts younger, decidedly non-hipster drinkers for honestly poured cocktails at fair prices.

After the death of her husband, owner Nancy Keane instituted a biweekly poetry series at the bar, which attracts readers from both the neighborhood and the wider Bay Area into this thin rail of a bar. Also, old-time music buffs can get their fiddle-and-banjo fix here on weekends.

Fans of horrific art need look no further than the portraits of two muscular Latina Amazons that hang above the bar, and a visit to the bathroom urine trough offers a wonderful view of a crudely painted mural of a blue-eyed vixen. Teetering alcoholics will likewise appreciate the handrails on the way to the men's room. Other attractions include Golden Tee, and the occasional mongrel wandering the bar for snacks and scratches behind the ear.

Those who like to toss one back first thing in the morning take note: The 33 opens at 7 a.m. Thursday through Sunday. The rest of the time it's 10 a.m.

Dive rating: ●●●●●●

3300 Club

Amnesia

853 Valencia St. (at 19th St.)
415-970-8336

Muni: 14, 26, 33, 49

Is this a dive, or does it just bear the ghost of one? Reincarnated in the space of the dearly departed Chameleon, Amnesia hasn't entirely forgotten what is in the echoes of its mind, try as it might. An ultra-red, artistically decorated bar that specializes in beer (20-plus micros on tap and dozens of Belgian ales in the bottle), Amnesia is a spiffed-up, less stanky version of the place where spilled beer once reigned supreme and Mission-bred poets came to try out their ragged lines.

In the back, on a raised stage where punk rock bands of old fired off assaults on drinkers' ears, a DJ now spins on some nights. On off nights, jukebox strains of punk split time with Curtis Mayfield, and the stage area offers a bird's-eye view of the pool table and candlelit tables below. Behind the copper-topped bar, an agreeable crew of bartenders makes change for a clientele that represents the new Mission: young, white, and fairly well off.

Despite the makeover, there's still plenty here to keep drink-oriented night owls happy. Most beers on tap are only $3, and there are also agave wine margaritas and sangria to sample. The motto at the top of the chalkboard says it all: "Some drink to remember, some drink to forget." Amnesia will never become the hipster haven that so many other neighborhood bars have become, but that's a good thing, as the Chameleon is probably rolling over in its grave in that cemetery where dead dives go to rest.

Dive rating:

Pabst Blue Ribbon (PBR) on tap

500 Club
Clooney's
Club 501
Kennedy's (Best deal in town: $5 pitchers)
La Rocca's
McKenzie's
Mission Bar
Rich's Club 93

500 Club

The Attic

3336 24th St. (at Mission St.)
415-643-3376

Muni: 14, 26, 48, 49, 67 • 24th St. BART station

There is no mystery to the gimmick here: old stuff. Tucked away above the bar or on the gallery shelves above the back room are knickknacks, trinkets, vintage furniture, old bikes, baseball bats, antique radios, toys, lamps . . . basically a treasure trove of odds and ends from decades ago. While you're sure to find plenty to look at as you sink into alcoholic oblivion, those who like their drinking spots more on the side of genuine grit may scoff at the tongue-in-chic décor here. At any rate, if the Attic ever goes under, make sure you catch the garage sale.

While its ads in the local weeklies have proclaimed it a dive, some may beg to differ. Whatever your definition, the Attic remains a dim and cozy little rail of a place with booths and tables in the back, and plenty of stools along the long bar. The bartenders are generally gorgeous and chatty, and the crowd is welcoming, aside from packed weekend nights when it's nearly impossible to order a drink or find a stool.

DJs occasionally bring in their decks to spin chill-out, down-tempo grooves, and live bands have also been known to show. While the crowd veers toward the hipster socialite, the place has yet to be overrun by bridge-and-tunnel weekend warriors. Drink prices are a wee bit on the high side, but keep in mind that every bar has its expenses, like taking out "dive bar" ads in the papers.

Dive rating:

Carlos Club

3278 24th St. (at Mission St.)
415-285-1512

Muni: 14, 26, 48, 49, 67 • 24th St. BART station

Curious train riders have long wondered about the place just outside the 24th Street BART station, whose fading advertisement has long beckoned with its "Commuters are welcome" and "Happy hours" tags. Usually a walk by the front door is enough to dissuade all but the most inquisitive. However, if you are brave enough to swallow your fear and go inside anyway, you will find the Carlos Club a seedy but not too threatening dive favored mainly by recent immigrants from Mexico and Central America.

Weekend afternoons can be just as busy as weekend nights, but if you're looking for the bar at its mellowest, stop in around midnight on any weeknight. Despite language barriers, you can probably make a friend or two in a short time. And if you happen to be a woman, you will make lots of friends — and you may very well drink for free. In addition to the migrant worker types, you'll also find a handful of grown-up gangbangers from the neighborhood's mean streets. Though the bar's vibe is fairly unthreatening, it's clear from the immense security guard that things can get out of hand from time to time. It's also clear that said immense security guard has established his place, since as soon as he bellows, "Last call," patrons make a run for it — not to the bar to get one for the road, but to the road itself.

If there were a San Francisco Museum of Dive Bar Art, the Carlos Club would be a member at the patron level. On the back wall, tandem murals of lusty dancing ladies — one of them a Latina vixen over a candle flame and the other a busty black woman with a cat looking up her skirt — offer wondrous visions for the drink-addled to ponder. Next to the antique wood bar is another fine painting of a topless Latina woman. These, and the two female bartenders, serve as the reminders of — or distractions from — the wives and lives many of the patrons left behind a thousand miles away.

A trip to the bathroom shouldn't be missed. The men's room is missing a doorknob, and those who enter step up onto redwood slats to protect their shoes from the standing water on the floor. A hardworking fan attempts to draw out the overwhelming scent of piss-soaked redwood, but alas, nothing can quite do that.

Dive rating: ●●●●●●●●

Clooney's

Muni: 14, 26, 48, 49, 67 • 24th St. BART station

Clooney's is one of those exceedingly rare bars where you can get a start before the proverbial cock crows. During any of the twenty hours a day when you can legally buy a drink in the state of California, you can buy one at Clooney's. One drinking buddy calls Clooney's his favorite place to come down from cocaine at 6 a.m., but we're not sure how much longer the comforting dinge and duff of yesteryear will hold out against the ravages of redecoration.

This longtime Mission pub is in essence a sports bar, one that in theme and temperament predates Barry Bonds, Pac Bell Park and satellite television. Here, it's pretty simple: a single TV above a horseshoe shaped bar. Relics of games past still line the walls: old Giants and Niners headlines ("Team of the '80s!"), a sign above the door pointing the way to Candlestick Park, and behind the bar, a purloined Kezar street sign (an ode to the 49ers old home, Kezar Stadium). These days, all the old decorations seem like window dressing as the bar hiccups through a series of new looks while trying not to offend its traditionalist daytime crew of oldster drinkers.

Gone are the old tiles, replaced by hardwood floors. A new pool table is a positive addition. Of debatable character are the Irish club tunes on the jukebox, making steady inroads against the stash of '70s rock, though our bartender promised that some of the old-timers would get up and shake it upon hearing their favorite techno anthem. This feisty Irish bar lass even tried to sell us on the merits of adding a "snuff room," which is a small cubbyhole with its own separate entrance, where womenfolk went to wait out their husbands' drinking sessions (or have a discreet tipple themselves) back in the old-country days when ladies were barred from bars. Ka-ching — can you say hipster magnet? I can't really say that a full-on makeover would be an improvement, but it is standard fare these days in the richer, trendier new Mission.

Drinks are cheap and poured strong, and the dedicated will find PBR on draft, although our bartender repeatedly tried to talk me out of drinking it. Another rare bonus, Clooney's is one of the few places to participate in that amazing thing called the buyback — where your bartender actually buys you a drink after you've emptied a few.

A sister bar to Harrington's in the Tenderloin (the dust-coated, working-class place on Larkin and Turk, not the yuppie-coated, no-class abyss on Front Street), Clooney's is a great place to suck a few down, or to sleep the night away after sucking one too many down. (One of our fellow patrons slept his way through the night without being 86'd.) Another patron, a heavy-metal tranny with the voice of John Wayne, told tales of sex, surgery, and success: "Dude, I've been through some serious shit."

Dive rating: 7, trying for 3 ●●●●●●●

Doc's Clock

Doc's Clock

2575 Mission St. (at 22nd St.)
415-824-3627

Muni: 12, 14, 26, 48, 49, 67 • 24th St. BART station

A harbinger of things to come, Doc's Clock cleaned up its act a few years back, transforming itself from genuine dive to a hipster's wet dream of one. Still, it remains a must-see booze venue for one reason alone: a marquee that would make Liberace proud. Flashing light bulbs, neon twisted into martini glasses, and the eternally true motto "cocktail time" beckon even those who don't like their strong sips delivered in stemmed glasses. Passing through the glass-cube semicircle of a doorway, however, those seeking a true to its roots, down-and-dirty dive will quickly be disappointed.

A long bar offers plenty of barstools to make acquaintance over, and in the back, plenty of tables bedecked by red candles — the common currency of the modern Mission bar — attract couples and groups of friends. One holdover from Doc's earlier era is the oft-used shuffleboard table against one wall. Drinks aren't exactly cheap, but they're poured strong enough to balance the currency exchange. Those too introverted to speak can ask the bartender for a dice cup and while the night away with games of liar's dice or Mexicali.

You may find that cut flowers and pink ceiling lights are enough to disqualify any bar from being a dive, and that's certainly true of the transformed former den of iniquity. But those who are drawn in by fabulous marquees and strong drinks may find that — hipsters or not — Doc's Clock is well aware that cocktail hour never ends.

Dive rating:

Double Play

2401 16th St. (at Bryant St.)
415-621-9859

Muni: 9, 12, 22, 27, 33, 53

It's a far cry from what most folks think of as a dive, but the Double Play is a San Francisco institution that any guide to drinking in San Francisco would be remiss to omit. Beloved by politicos, developers, newspaper editors, reporters, and others who occasion to talk business over a three-martini lunch, the Double Play has been getting folks sauced during daylight hours since 1909. It's also a hangout for burly working folks, neighborhood hipsters, and baseball fans with a hankering for history.

Baseball, not surprisingly, is at the heart of the Double Play, which once stood in the shadow of Seals Stadium, home of San Francisco's Pacific Coast League baseball team from 1931 to 1957. (In true San Francisco fashion, that fabled ballpark fell decades back to be redeveloped into something entirely more garish — now it's a strip mall of Safeway, Gap, Ross, Old Navy, Boston Market, and other Chains-R-Us outfitters.) The Double Play's got sports ephemera going back nearly a century: old mitts, photos, pennants, etc. If you love baseball and think there wasn't life before the Giants migrated from New York in 1957 (to play two seasons at Seals Stadium), pay this place a visit.

Busy at the lunch hour, the bar does brisk business at happy hour on game days. There are no specials, but domestic drafts are $2.50, so who's complaining? Food is a bit pricey — in the $10 range for Italian dishes. But there's a cheap Chinese place down the street that will deliver right to your barstool after the kitchen's closed.

Dive rating:

Dovre Club

Things just aren't the same. It used to be that this neighborhood Irish dive occupied a small corner of the Women's Building on 18th Street, leading many to revere this curious coexistence as some grand sign of everyone's ability to get along. Local lefty politicos and neighborhood drunks alike savored an ancient drink tank within spitting distance of female drum therapy workshops and battered women's clinics. However, one seismic upgrade and eviction later, the Dovre is on its own, forced to relocate to a nondescript stretch of Valencia.

In the new location, some of the old character is gone — no big surprise in the New Mission. But the Dovre Club remains a neighborhood pub with a dedicated following of hard-drinking regulars. While one can certainly find a more authentic Irish experience in the Richmond or elsewhere in the Mission, this corner bar has oodles of Emerald character. Two long rooms separated by a bar with two countertops, the place is a lively cacophony of trash-talking drinking buddies. There's also a pool table and decent jukebox with some choice opportunities for mixing it up.

If you make a trip to the toilet, look up for a bewildering view of an old sailor captain portrait painting. The effect is significantly better after a shot or two of Jameson.

Dive rating:

El Amigo

A draw for young, male Latinos, this outer Mission corner bar packs them in, but only because it's *so* tiny. How tiny is it? It's so tiny that if you're able to get a seat at the bar, you'll end up with bruises on your back from errant pool cues, as the place is scarcely larger than its single pool table. Newcomers may get suspicious glances as they walk through the door, but it's probably because everyone else is wondering if you'll actually fit inside the place. However, if you can make drunk-talk en español, you'll be king in no time. King of what, I don't know, as the lonely hombres seem to be here to do what lonely hombres everywhere usually do — drown their cares, play forlorn ballads on the jukebox, and ogle the cute bar lasses.

Drinks are cheap, unless you order name liquors. If you do, we recommend a gin and tonic — they glow beautifully in the otherwise unnoticeable black lights above the bar. Beers are $2.50, and lots of Mexican brands are offered. The décor consists primarily of wooden yard screening tacked to all of the walls, the type of stuff you slap to an ugly fence in order to hide it. There are also a handful of half-blown strings of Christmas lights strung up haphazardly, the Mission District's answer to mood lighting. At any rate, the place is so damned small that you're unlikely to notice anything other than the back of someone's head right in front of you.

The bar is connected to the favorite hipster dive restaurant, Emmy's Spaghetti Shack, where 40s of Mickey's come served in ice buckets and the house special is, you guessed it, spaghetti and meatballs. Due to the restaurant's tiny size and huge popularity, El Amigo frequently serves as its spillover room, offering hipsters yet another opportunity to rub elbows with the fading Mexican character of the Mission.

Dive rating: ●●●●●●●●

Il Pirata

Woe to the Friday afternoon drink seeker who doesn't work at UPS, for the brown-clad hordes take over from the first clock-out until the last of them stumbles out into the night. If you throw caution to the wind and decide that fifty or so drunken delivery drivers are your ideal drinking companions, be prepared to discover a corporate culture more game room than mailroom. High-stakes liars dice, shots of Hennessy and expensive tequila, plus loads of hootin' and hollerin', are just some of the TGIF revelry that the brown are known to engage in. A few Friday evenings here, and you might just want a job at UPS.

In many respects, though, the UPS happy hour is only one of the many personalities Il Pirata seems to have. One side of the place is occupied by an Italian restaurant, where enormous fans blow over plush black booths, and the food isn't bad or pricey. The other side is the domain of the bar, a cozy old wooden monument with glass-faced refrigerated racks holding bottles and glasses so you can see how cold your beer is. While the bar stocks a strong selection of tequilas, whiskies, and other assorted finer drinking pleasures for Friday's big spenders, it's also a place for a $2.50 bottle of Bud.

It's true dive heaven when the multiple TVs are turned down and the hazy air clears a bit, but Il Pirata can be sports central when a big game's on. On some nights, the restaurant is transformed into a low-key nightclub, with DJs spinning and hipsters trying to look cool in a dumpy Italian place.

Dive rating: ●●●●●●

Jack's Club

Just a few steps from San Francisco General Hospital, Jack's is a basic but cozy little Mexican bar. In the style of our Southern neighbor, your beer (cans of Tecate, bottled Negra Modelo, and other Mexi favorites) comes with a dish of big fat lime quarters. To the uninitiated, it's an odd combination, but a little lime squeeze goes a long way, and it's likely you'll be asking your favorite bartender for a wedge with your next pop.

This place is as far from the new Mission as you're going to get. No gel-coiffed hipsters here; not a leather-encased trip-hop freak to be found. It's just a few Mexican guys and maybe an older couple slow-dancing on the linoleum to something on the jukebox. The place appears to be a converted flat, and its feel is certainly homey. There's not much to look at — just you in the mirror behind the bar, a couple jars of pickled vegetables, and the jovial bartender as she cracks open another Tecate.

Vintage game aficionados will find Show Boat and Triple Play by way of entertainment, and a couple of perpetually silent TVs provide visual stimulation. Guitar fetishists can drop quarters for ex-Mission homeboy Santana and fellow SFers Metallica on the jukebox.

It's the perfect place to wait for your cousin to come out of surgery at the hospital. The familiar drunken smile on your face will be the first thing he sees, and then he will know that everything is going to be all right.

Dive rating: ● ● ● ● ● ● ●

Jay & Bee

2736 20th St. (at York St.)
415-824-4190

Muni: 9, 27, 33

Sitting inside this tragically empty hole, you get the feeling you've gone back in time to the Mission District of the 1940s. Laquered tables, misted-glass windows on either side of the door, a column sheathed in fancy leather, and the bright neon sign above the door make Jay & Bee the real deal. The problem is the patrons, or more precisely, lack of patrons, all of whom appear to have stepped out for a smoke on that warm night in 1947, and never stepped back in.

Jay & Bee has been a neighborhood fixture for better than fifty years. Once the home away from home for cops, firemen, and construction workers, the bar used to offer weekend meals, and during hard times, even pitched in free meals for those down on their luck. A turnover in ownership a few years back has led to the bar's slow fade. While there are still some cool touches — the authentic retro feel, the terminally strong cocktails, the smoking patio in the rear — it's hard to imagine life in San Francisco would be any different without this place. Without a pool table, jukebox, or good-looking patrons, Jay & Bee doesn't offer much to attract newcomers other than its fading history.

If you do stumble across this place, which you're not likely to do given its off-the-beaten-whatever locale, you're liable not to run into anyone but a bored bartender and perhaps a slightly lost couple seeking strength before moving on to the Monkey Club or some other nearby boozery. And, with fairly sporadic operating hours, Jay & Bee is also a place you might think twice about before trekking across town to visit. Wednesdays to Saturdays are usually good, Tuesday's a mystery, and Sunday and Monday are never on. Let the neon marquee be your guide — if it's on, you can probably get your mojo tuned up here.

For $200, you can also rent the place for a private party. You still have to pay for drinks, but the bar will chase out potential party crashers. Not that there will be any.

Dive rating:

Kilowatt

3160 16th St. (at Albion St.)
415-861-2595

Muni: 14, 22, 26, 33, 49, 53
6th St. BART station

Once the stomping ground of punks, bike messengers, and the motorcycle crowd, the Kilowatt has gotten a haircut, taken out the nose ring, and upgraded its new wardrobe. The clients have anyway, even if the bar is still dingy and scuffed enough to let folks feel like they're slumming. While it remains a slice of what 16th & Valencia used to be like before the area become the It-strip four nights a week, this part of the Mission has changed, and there is no going back.

Even so, you'll still find a few pierced and tattooed stragglers angling around the pool tables and sipping on microbrews, the 'Watt's specialty. There are seventeen beers on tap, most priced around $3.50, and a dozen or so bottled beers. Mixed drinks come high-octane here as well. Happy hour swilling can bring your drinking budget down a hair, with most pints priced at $2.50.

Perhaps due to the steady flow of B&T weekenders, the Kilowatt is a lot friendlier than some of the other biker/punk beer bars like the Zeitgeist or the Toronado. If you don't get served here, it's not because the bartender's an asshole, it's because he's working his ass off. Despite its hectic weekend pace, the bar does have a crew of regulars who come in, sometimes bringing a dog or two to wander the room, sniff patrons' crotches, and crawl below barstools for stray pieces of burrito or pizza. A Polaroid gallery behind the bar might help you recognize some of the regulars in your midst.

In the back of the bar is a raised platform where punk bands once shredded eardrums. A sign of a changing musical climate, the Kilowatt ditched live music years ago, only to be followed by a number of other small venues across the city. Now you can grab a table on the old stage and watch the action from a better vantage point. Even without a band, the decibel level on a busy night can only be described as earsplitting, with raucous drunken conversations (read: yelling) competing with a deafening jukebox.

Dive rating: ● ● ● ● ●

La Rondalla

Famous for its margaritas and mariachis, La Rondalla attracts a fairly mainstream crowd during meal hours, when huge platters of sit-down style Mexican food offer an alternative to the neighborhood's ubiquitous taquerias. A permanent combination of Yuletide ode and tribute to those Latino stars of yesteryear, this bar/restaurant is continuously bedecked in Christmas lights, poinsettias, silver tinsel, balloons, and other genuine kitsch, and the back room is packed with portraits of famed Latina leading ladies from times long gone.

With a bar clientele that's mostly middle-aged Latino men, as well as the occasional couple, La Rondalla is a quiet place for sipping beer or margaritas by the pitcher and listening to the Beatles and lonely Mexican love ballads on the jukebox. On slow nights when the kitchen has closed, La Rondalla transforms itself from San Francisco eating institution to neighborhood dive. At $11 a pitcher, the margaritas are a fucking bargain, and potent to boot. Be advised that the well tequila is likely to linger with you for at least twenty-four hours. Cheap booze aficionado DJ Gravy said he had to scrape the taste out of his mouth with Jager shots the next night. So if you're worried, make it Cuervo for an extra couple bucks. Mixed drinks are similar bargains, and La Rondalla stocks a full selection of Mexican beer at honest prices.

Despite the unassuming vibe, the wild side can sneak in from time to time. On a recent cold and windy weeknight, a pair of off-duty hookers, who had struck out trying to pick-up one of the bar's lonely drinkers, started to give each other backrubs and hugs at the bar. One thing led to another, and their pimp eventually convinced them to swap spit for the titillating benefit of everyone at the bar. Even the beefy security guard seemed amused and didn't bother to 86 either the streetwalkers or their main man.

Dive rating: 4 at 8 p.m.; 8 at midnight

Latin American Club

3286 22nd St. (at Valencia St.)
415-647-2732

Muni: 14, 26, 48, 49, 67
24th St. BART station

You won't find any Latin Americans here, hombre, but that doesn't mean you can't put on your shiniest pair of black-framed glasses and some kind of oddball hat and blend in with the hordes of Mission hipsters who call the Latin American home. Even if it seems that the cool kids' bus broke down in front, you'll still find an empty table or barstool to call your own on most weeknights. In spite of itself, the Latin American is actually a decent place to suck down one or ten.

The décor inside appears to be the result of a lifetime of combing through garage sales. Tables and chairs are fittingly retro. Antiquated wooden snowshoes share a wall with an enormous animal skin. One wall is something of a cuckoo clock hall of fame. Piñatas, Mexican banners, and strings of Christmas lights adorn the ceiling. Art — hipster art, natch — garnishes the wall opposite the bar. A personal favorite is the immense poster unraveling the mysteries of placental circulation, circa 1950s sex ed.

Rumor has it that the bar's specialty is the margarita, and from the number of salted glasses circulating the room, it's probably damn tasty. Those with serious fear of tequila can opt for standard cocktails or a variety of semi-obscure microbrews on tap, a few of which you're unlikely to find anywhere else in the city. While the young, stylish, and raucous clientele would certainly drive any self-respecting old salt to drink, you're quite unlikely to find any grizzled graybeards doing so here.

Dive rating: ●●●●●

PBR in bottle or can

Fulton Street
Grant & Green
The Odeon
Phone Booth
XS
Zeitgeist

Mission Bar

2965 Mission St. (at 23rd St.)
415-647-2300

Muni: 12, 14, 26, 48, 49, 67
24th St. BART station

One by one, the Mission's once numerous dives are being eclipsed by nouveau hip versions of what they once were. However, the march of progress has been halted at Mission Bar, or Bar as it's more frequently known. Here, your quest for Pabst Blue Ribbon on tap will find its answer, and those with wealthier tastes will find Bass, Guinness, Anchor Steam, and Sierra by the pint. Well drinks are as cheap and strong as they should be, and the service is as nice as it needs to be. Many of the area's bars remain ethnically divided, but Bar attracts a mixed neighborhood crowd of Anglos and Latinos.

Perhaps because it's rarely crowded, Bar's door is always wide open, allowing cigarette smoke and flower sellers to drift in and out almost unnoticed beneath a black sign with oversize red letters with the simple invitation: "BAR." Inside, you'll find a barstool with your name on it, as well as a handful of black Naugahyde booths from which to take in the bipolar décor (half old beer posters and half devil- or Day of the Dead-related pictures). Other amenities include a pool table in back, a jukebox that mixes salsa and funk, and the hallmark of a true dive: the nastiest men's room you'll ever come across.

Dive rating: ●●●●●●●

Mission Bar

Nap's Only

Nap's Only

3152 Mission St. (at Precita Ave.)
415-648-1226

Muni: 12, 14, 26, 27, 33, 49, 67

A couple doors down, neighborhood hot spot El Rio bills itself as "your dive." If that's the case, Nap's is "our dive," the place where the rest of us go when we don't want to pay a cover, dance to world music, or watch independent films project onto the patio wall. A cozy, intimate dive in the truest sense of the word, Nap's is a microcosm of the Mission that everybody loves and nobody wants to admit doesn't exist in many places anymore. Whether it's the dim lighting, the failing Christmas lights, or the faded Victorian wallpaper, Nap's invites you in for a drink on the premise that you might move in for a lifetime.

Drinks are cut-rate and extremely potent. If you order cocktails, they come in tall and short, a concept I wish more bars would adopt. There's a pool table in back, and a patio from which one could lob rotten tomatoes at the patrons in the back patio at El Rio, if one were so inclined. A large portion of the regulars speak Spanish, and many of them are long-time Mission residents as opposed to newcomers, which gives the bar a delightfully lived-in feel. There are photos of all kinds of children behind the bar — neighborhood kids, soccer teams, the whole family vibe. Many of these photos are yellowed and dog-eared, old enough that you may in fact be sitting next to the grown-up original of one of them. The bar brings together a rare mix: young singles, semi-retired gang-bangers, older couples, lonely old men, lost bar hoppers, and other seemingly out-of-place folks. Somehow, they're all in place at Nap's.

I'm normally not a big fan of karaoke, especially in a town where dedi-cated karaoke bars attract singers with talent, who sing in order to impress their friends. That's not the case at karaoke night at Nap's, where nobody sings until they're drunk enough to do it, and by the time they're drunk enough to do it, there's slim chance of doing it well. In other words, sheer entertainment in a not entirely laughing-with-you sort of way.

Dive rating:

The Odeon

While the boho/artist scene that spawned Burning Man and other freaky occurrences came close to death during the dot-com era, a small bit of it thankfully lives on at the Odeon. The latest endeavor of post-punk carnie Chicken John is a nonstop freak show of oddball events, strange programming, and general drunken revelry. For those not in the know, Chicken John was (quite briefly) a bandmate of punk-rock über-rebel G.G. Allin, and later went on to infamy in Burning Man, Circus Redickuless, Tentacle Sessions, and umpteen dozen other shows, scams, hoaxes, and jokes. This ultimate prankster has even confessed to impersonating 23-year-old Asian hotties on Craigslist in order to attract business ("Meet me at the Odeon . . .").

The Odeon might just be Chick's last laugh. Among the clientele you'll find plenty of artiste-types who clearly feel in on the joke, as well as goatee-sporting, beret-wearing older folks. There are also assorted hipster and college-aged kids looking for a weird night out. They'll usually get one. While it's clear a huge wad of money didn't go into decorations, a tremendous amount of time did. From the front end of a classic car embedded above the old-school bar, to the papier-mâché squid in the corner, to the mysterious animal skeleton hung at one end of the place, there's plenty to look at here — even if the show's a stinker. But be aware that those who remain apathetic to Chick's attempts at a night's good fun may be invited to check out the more ersatz Argus Lounge a few doors down Mission Street.

The uninitiated may want to give the Odeon a try on Wednesday night for Ask Dr. Hal, in which Chick and frequent collaborator Dr. Howland Owll answer stupid (and serious) questions of any variety for small bills. Those who come up with the best questions — or at least the ones Chicken John likes the best — earn themselves a free shot of some odd liquor that's not selling very well at the bar. On other evenings, there's live music from local and art-haus bands, bad karaoke night, and whatever else Chick dreams up. It's likely to be strange or interesting, if not both. While the drinks aren't cheap, at least the show is usually free. After a few $3 Buds, you might even be ready to try the Hal Robins Martini — a Pabst Blue Ribbon with an olive.

Dive rating:

Phone Booth

1398 S. Van Ness Ave. (at 25th St.)
415-648-4683

Muni: 12, 14, 26, 27, 48, 49, 67
24th St. BART station

It may not have the same cachet as most of the trendy Mission bars, but the Phone Booth manages to pack them in seven nights a week despite its off-the-path locale and miniscule drinking quarters. While the coolish clientele can turn this low-key place into a hipster circus (you're guaranteed to see somebody wearing a battered cowboy hat), it's hardly an exclusive watering hole unless the bartender is giving you a hard time, which has been known to happen.

Expect a mixed crowd of couples, gays and lesbians, lonely hipsters, and musician-types sporting Keith Richards haircuts. My friend Boris says he stumbled in on a roomful of ladies one night after a few drinks, with a barcrawler's rocket in his pocket. It took him a drink or two to realize that it was lesbian night and the icy stares were his invitation to take his tattered libido elsewhere. That said, on most nights, the place is filled with all sorts of people tossing wanton glances about, and it's tiny enough that you're bound to spill your drink on plenty of people by way of introduction.

The thrift-store décor is a bit overdone — with a black velvet bullfighter painting on the wall, 1960s-era lamps everywhere, and a signed picture of Tom Selleck behind the bar. One admirable piece of decoration is the lamp above the bar, fashioned primarily out of Barbie dolls. Music aficionados will appreciate the eclectic juke selection, mixing '80s pop and cheese rock with a smattering of current indie artists. Despite its too-earnest attempts at becoming a hipster dive, the Phone Booth has a certain charm — and the $5 shot of Jack with a PBR chaser is enough to warm even the most jaded dive aficionado.

Dive rating: ●●●●●●

Phone Booth

Rite Spot Café

THE MISSION/BERNAL HEIGHTS

A bit off the beaten path from most Mission District hot spots, the Rite Spot requires a bit of dedication to find, as well as a stroll through one of the neighborhood's dingier stretches. But once you've arrived, you'll find, inside a scrappy, nondescript corner building, one of San Francisco's best bars. Slightly more upscale than many of the other establishments in this book (white tablecloths, food, local art on the walls, neo-boho musicians playing ragtime, jazz, or vaudeville), the Rite Spot, however, is still able to pass the bathroom filth test that determines a dive's true worth, as its restrooms are as graffiti- and sticker-coated as any other (though its scent is far more urinal-disk than real piss on the floor).

I first stumbled across the place when my drink-tipping, photo-clicking buddy Greg had an exhibition showing. Since then, I've dragged friend after friend the six or so blocks over from the Mission's busier Valencia drinking strip to the one bar that hasn't lost an essence of the old San Francisco that is becoming increasingly hard to find. Draft beer and cocktails are a bit steeper than dive-rate, but there's always Bud in the bottle for the budget drinker. The menu is comprised primarily of pasta dishes, and is fair-priced at between $8 and $10 for a generous plate. If you want to get a candlelit view of your date, grab a table. If your date just doesn't do the trick, fill your aesthetic void by taking in the cocktail napkin art gallery behind the antique cash register, or the artistic types that make up the primary clientele and remind one of a Mission that once was and looks to be not much more.

Local history buffs and smokers with three minutes to kill ought to wander down 17th Street a half block to see the old Mission Police Station, a stately marble palace whose services have been replaced by the newer, larger, and far less glamorous station on Valencia.

SAN FRANCISCO'S BEST DIVE BARS

Dive rating:

Rite Spot Café

Sadie's Flying Elephant

491 Potrero Ave. (at Mariposa St.)
415-551-7988

Muni: 9, 22, 27, 33, 53

One of the best things about San Francisco is the fact that on any given night, you can wander the streets and find a multitude of chairs, tables, lamps, and other assorted pieces of junk, I mean furniture, that the city's apartment dwellers have decided to cast away. During spring-cleaning season especially, the city can feel like an Ikea without walls. Unfortunately, the pickin's have become a bit slimmer in the immediate neighborhood of Sadie's, as the place appears intent upon beating the Sanitation Department to the city's unwanted relics.

A cavernous place tucked away in what from the outside looks like a tiny Potrero Street storefront, Sadie's has become a favorite for hipster-types living on the edge of the Mission. Foam-hemorrhaging couches and easy chairs, scarred pool tables, and a dilapidated but serviceable pop-corn machine define the bar's dingy aesthetics. The back room has been painted with chalkboard-style black paint, inviting patrons to take up chalk and scrawl their own versions of art, slander, or something in between. It's a nice idea, if only one could easily erase the layers of drunken detritus beneath each generation of graffiti.

While it's a friendly place where you have a decent shot at nabbing a pool table for an hour or two, plan on male bonding if you're a guy, or if you're a woman, having your pick of the litter here — on most nights, Sadie's is one big sausage fest. And, it is a rummage-fest every night. Case in point: On my last visit, a guy asked me if I'd seen his toilet seat. Before I'd even had a chance to answer, he picked it up off the floor beside me and proudly carried it around for the rest of the night.

Dive rating:

Sadie's Flying Elephant

Thieves Tavern

3349 20th St. (at Shotwell St.)
415-401-8661

Muni: 12, 14, 49

I first went to this place after a Giants game at the 'stick, after my friend Pete circled through blocks and blocks of an obscure residential section of the Mission looking for a bar he remembered going to once, but had obviously forgotten where. It was called the Shotwell back then, and it was a bit rougher around the edges, a place where bike messengers, dogs, and neighborhood freaks would come to toss trash over pool, pints, and free popcorn, back in the days when you could still smoke in bars. And smoke Pete and I did that night.

The Shotwell is no more, but Thieves will be a smoker's joint till cancer comes. As an owner-operated bar, Thieves is legally exempt from the smoking ban enforced throughout the state. Thus the air has that old-time carcinogenic aroma. Sure, there's plenty of places in San Francisco that'll let you curl up a beer coaster and pull a furtive drag from time to time. But guilt-free, legal smoking . . . oh, how sweet it used to be.

Drawing a largely male, beer-swilling crowd of Mission locals, it's a neighborhood place that's impossibly hard to find, especially if you've got a buzz on. There's no sign, few lights, and a languid jukebox with healthy respect for its neighbors. Thieves' other charms come in its dark, cozy feel, a couple of well-used pool tables, and a memorable old wooden bar to gaze at from your wrought-iron stool. It's got history, legions of dedicated drinkers, a deliciously regrettable name, and guilt-free ashtrays. Some would call it heaven. But I still call it the Shotwell.

Dive rating:

Treat Street

Along a sketchy gang-owned strip of 24th Street, Treat Street is a comfortably dingy oasis of friendly neighborhood inebriation. You'll recognize it from a block or two away by the beer lights posted on the walls. Drawing aging hipsters, working-class folks, Mission artsy people, and the occasional druggie, there's always something a little bit on the down-low going on here. But don't let that get in the way of your buzz, or the welcoming chitchat you're likely to encounter, particularly if you hang at the bar with the hard-drinking regulars. On my most recent visit, I discussed retirement housing plans with a woman who was dead set against her grandkids moving in with her. Ever.

PETA members and vegetarians may want to head elsewhere, as the enviable gallery of taxidermied animals is a who's who of interesting dead stuff: the usual deer and elk, an owl, turtle, mountain goat, pheasant, and even a boar with upended shot glasses on its tusks. Near the pool table hang large ocean-going fish swimming a perpetual circle around the room. While conversation at Treat Street is usually loud and heavily inflected in drunklish, the jukebox is louder and heavily accented in rock and roll: AD/DC, Thin Lizzy, Stones, etc.

The back room pool table may be slightly crooked, but it's frequently unused. Treat Street's men's room is possibly the most graffiti-coated bathroom in the entire city, and its piss-soaked floor is an offering to the dive bar gods themselves. Check out the Polaroid booth; you may just want to leave a picture of yourself in the bar's photo gallery, if the bartender will oblige you.

From Treat Street, you're within a brushstroke of Balmy Alley, San Francisco's world-famous open-air gallery of murals. Some of them are decades old, others brand-new. All of them draw on the neighborhood's rich history of political and activist street art. You can easily walk across 24th Street and catch a glance of some of the work during a smoke break.

Dive rating:

Uptown

200 Capp St. (at 17th St.)
415-861-8231

Muni: 12, 14, 22, 33, 49, 53 • 16th St. BART station

With high ceilings, painted wainscoting, and a curio shelf that runs the perimeter of the room, the Uptown has the feel of a slumlord's San Francisco dream apartment. That sense is magnified by the ratty couches near the bathrooms and a woefully inefficient and outdated gas heater — the same one I have in my apartment. Hell, I've even run into my upstairs neighbor here, and this is a guy who drinks all day while writing terrible poetry and yells all night. Any place he drinks should have his picture on the wall under a sign that says, "This is a dive."

A favorite for Mission dwellers and those tired of Valencia's more perennially packed bars, the Uptown charms with its low-key ambiance and honestly priced drinks. Offering about ten micros on tap, lots of bottled beer, and cocktail creations (nothin' fancy, champ), the Uptown draws some rough-around-the-edges locals and a handful of couples out for drinks and flirtatious conversation. On weekends and busy nights, the crowd can veer toward the "cleaner, whiter, brighter" side of the new Mission, but you'll still find some oldsters chatting up the bartenders and checking out the face of the new neighborhood that's growing up around them.

Most people opt for one of the booths, where springs poke through the seats to make pincushions of asses and the Formica tabletops bear multiple generations of graffiti. You can also expect a very personal sniff from one of the dogs that frequently wander the grounds. Other notable attractions include a fantastic jukebox, an always busy pool table, a cheesy mural above the couches, and one of the sickest bathrooms — graffiti-coated urine trough and all — this side of Waco.

Neighborhood characters sometimes walk through the doors, as flower vendors and the occasional tamale lady (and not uncommonly, *the* Tamale Lady) wander in to sell their wares. Outside on the street, keep an eye out for other neighborhood characters, as you're only a couple blocks from one of the city's busy strips for low-rent hookers.

Dive rating: ●●●●●●

Wild Side West

True to its name, the Wild Side conjures up the essence of a century-old saloon, with deep red paint on the walls, well worn wooden floorboards, and . . . naked women art on every conceivable portion of available wall and ceiling space. OK, so maybe it's a lesbian version of the frontier tavern, but it's a downright fine place to stop in for a drink on quaint Cortland Ave.

While it's certainly a bar for ladies who love ladies, the Wild Side's vibe is welcoming and mellow for almost everyone. Men, straight couples, and random neighborhood folks all stop in at what is basically just a cool neighborhood bar that caters to lesbians. The place has a homey vibe, with a brick fireplace in the center of the room, a very popular pool table right at the entrance, and artwork and masks from far corners of the earth. The cash register is genuine old saloon style — as is the collection of aged lamps above the bar.

One of the major draws is the back patio and garden. Open until 10 p.m., the garden is a little slice of greenery offering tucked-away seats and other crevices to explore after a few strong drinks. The smoking patio is open until closing time.

Dive rating:

Zeitgeist

No self-respecting beer snob can call his life complete without a trip to Zeitgeist, the champion of all beer bars in San Francisco. Local breweries are well represented, and you're likely to find some here you won't find anywhere else. Those with more refined tastes can request a lukewarm bottle of Pabst to cuddle their lips against. This is a full bar though, and one with its advantages — order a double and you'll get it in a pint glass so you don't waste time making extra trips to the bar.

Inside, you'll find all the crooked, dirty tables you want, a pool table, two filthy bathrooms, and some of the most gorgeous punk rock bartenders to ever pour a pint (both boys and girls). Most folks order a pitcher (one of the few places in the city where you'll find them) and head for the back patio. It's set up like a German beer garden with long rows of picnic tables, where strangers become friends and friends become stranger all the time. On sunny afternoons, it's a madhouse of drunken conversation and happy smokers. At night, it's still frequently crowded, but there's a bit more room to move. It's the kind of place where your buddy can stick his head between two tables and discreetly barf his brains out without offending anyone. I know that because my friend Mudfoot did just that the last time he was in town.

Two-wheeled drinking enthusiasts, whether they ride a Moto Guzzi V7 Special or a duct-tape encased track bike with no brakes, are also in the majority here, along with the beer lovers. Such an intersection can provide hours of entertainment, as pint-toting yuppie brew buffs try to edge in for another beer between two tattooed, pierced bike messengers. While its punk/biker credentials are still solid, the clientele is less wallet chain and more Dockers khaki these days.

In the evenings, there's standard pub grub in the back of the bar, and on sunny Sundays, the barbecue action moves out to the back patio. The food's OK, but the beer always improves the quality. Another benefit is that Zeitgeist also runs a hostel/hotel upstairs from the bar, with pretty cheap rates on rooms. The downside is living upstairs from a bar; the upside is . . . living upstairs from a bar. Inquire within during afternoon hours.

Dive rating: ●●●●●

Best Jukeboxes

Cassidy's
Crow Bar
Fulton Street
The Hearth
Lucky 13
Zeitgeist

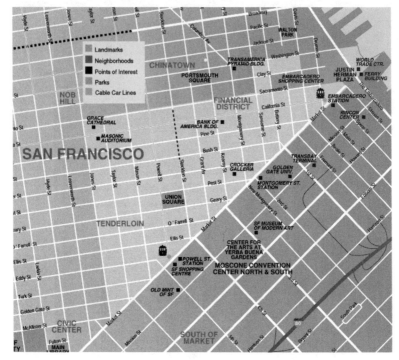

Union Square

NOB HILL/
UNION SQUARE

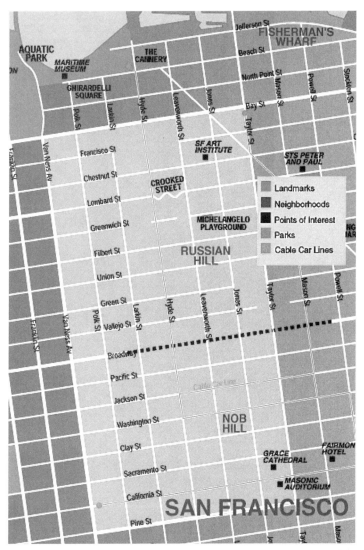

Nob Hill

Bacchus Kirk

There was an old-timer, rest his soul, who was so addicted to Triple Play, that hallowed 1950s precursor to pinball, that he would take the bus down from Santa Rosa to play one of the two machines at Bacchus Kirk on weekends. After the bar closed for the night, he'd head down the hill back to his hotel room in the Tenderloin, where his dreams were only of one thing: his next date with Triple Play. The story goes that he spent his last few weekends racking up numbers at Triple Play — it's no game of skill, just of luck, sort of like bingo in the shape of a pinball machine. When one of the bartenders hassled him about dropping so much cash into the machine, he spat back, "Fuck you, there's a pussy inside this game!" Needless to say, he was left alone to spend his last few days and dollars with the mistress he loved. He lives no longer, but his Triple Play still waits for a newly determined gamesman to step up for some action.

That's only part of the lore of Bacchus Kirk, a lower Nob Hill neighborhood spot with tons of character, in a multiple personality disorder sort of way. Fish tanks, a moose head above the bar, a dangling disco ball, an easy chair by the door, tavern knickknacks ad infinitum, pencil-drawn caricatures tacked to the ceiling — it's hard to say what the defining element is. But whatever it is, it works, because the place has been a local favorite for years. Even the bar itself is worn down to the wood from the eons of bottles and glasses that have slid across its surface. On a street with a bar (or two) every block, Kirk's has long been tops.

There's no beer on tap, but bottle prices are cheap. The drinks are efficient, to get to the point. While you won't always find a crowd, if you're looking for one on Bush Street, try here first. The regulars are largely made up of the attractive Nob Hill element, not your usual dive bar clientele. And if the conversation sucks, the jukebox doesn't, so grab a buck and stick it somewhere that feels good.

Dive rating:

C Bobby's Owl Tree

601 Post St. (at Taylor St.)
415-776-9344

Muni: 2, 3, 4, 27; Powell cable cars

The Owl Tree has been a Nob Hill institution for twenty-five years, managed with smooth efficiency by a white-haired gentleman named Bobby (I don't know where he got the C from). Many would hesitate to call the Owl Tree a dive, and I can't technically disagree with them. But in a neighborhood of crappy tourist traps and overpriced hotel bars, Bobby's is an old-school joint that'll have you pining for the days of cigar smoke and red meat. A free bowl of Chex party mix comes with every order, and the bar has yet to upgrade to a tonic/soda/Coke fountain for mixed drinks. Bobby pours his generous G&Ts and Jack and Cokes straight from the bottle or can. The men's room urinal, its ceramic basin ceremoniously stocked with ice, offers the rare San Fran sensation of peeing in the snow. Sorry girls, no such thrill awaits you in the ladies' room up the narrow stairs.

Every square inch of the tiny corner bar is covered in namesake paraphernalia of some sort: etched glass owls, owl paintings, owl photos, ceramic owls, macramé owls, the enormous stained glass owl behind the bar . . . you get the picture. Actually, you can't possibly get the picture unless you see the place for yourself. It's a truly amazing sight.

Over the years, I've experienced some strange and unpredictable evenings at the Owl Tree. Like the time we met a former barback who had pulled up a stool and several highballs in order to reflect on his teenage years helping at the bar decades earlier. He bought many drinks for many people, hit on most everyone (indiscriminate of sex or sexual orientation), and even offered to drive us to New Orleans, tonight, if only we'd go have a nightcap with him in the trunk of his car. We had other plans.

Dive rating: ●●●●●●

Chelsea Place

641 Bush St. (at Stockton St.)
415-989-2524

Muni: 2, 3, 4, 30, 45; Powell cable cars

When I worked in the Financial District, there was a seedy little dive above the Stockton Tunnel that often interrupted my walk home. Then one day this seedy little dive was transformed into a yuppie drinking academy, so I kept on walking along Bush. Luckily, I had to walk only a few doors down to run into Chelsea Place, the perfect happy hour spot to while away my post-work blues.

Run with cool efficiency by a kindly Asian bar lady named Jennifer (and her cute staff), this is the kind of place to go after you've been thrown on the scrap heap of existence by your ex. The music is low-key, the walls adorned with bad art and beer posters, and the conversation is kept to a minimum. While it's often populated by solo drinkers who love to tell dull stories, Chelsea occasionally, due to its close proximity to a zillion nearby hotels, attracts groups who pack into the back booth by the fireplace, and may, if you are real lucky, treat you to air guitar symphonies, bar-top drum solos, or endless playings of "Brown-Eyed Girl." Fortunately, most of the Van Morrison wanna-bes guzzle their drinks and beat a quick exit, leaving you to quietly appreciate the fact that being dumped may, at times, not be such a bad thing.

Dive rating:

Overflo

The name might suggest that this is a place where everybody shows up when their favorite spot is too crowded. But it actually refers to your drink, or more accurately, the way your drink is poured. Mike, the gravel-throated bartender, pours his libations and then pours some more, until it spills over the top of the glass onto the counter, creating a delightful mess to the jaded dive bar eye. And, he's even been known to warm up a half-empty cocktail or two for those who like them extra fortified.

From the faded old uniforms tacked up behind the bar and the flags and yellowing military photographs on the wall, it's clear this is a place dedicated to men in uniform, or at least once was. Today, Overflo is just a place for working stiffs: guys in paint-spattered pants, fellas with nametags on their shirts (no, not those ironic hipsters), and mustachioed off-duty cops. It also gets some out-of-towners slumming it from the hotels down Sutter Street, and a steady stream of the TL's best barflies. The lure, as always, is the cheap brain lube, the blue-collar atmosphere, and its associated crowd with whom to get drunk.

Mike, who told me his next quest was to get Pabst on tap, has plenty of stories to tell. Plenty of stories — getting him to stop telling them can be the problem. If you're not into talk, head to the glassed-in pool room, where you can shoot a game or dangle your arm out the door to smoke.

Dive rating:

Summer Place

801 Bush St. (at Mason St.)
415-441-2252

Muni: 2, 3, 4, 27; Powell cable cars

If you want to go out for a drink without feeling like you've left your apartment, this newcomer on Bush's booze alley will accomplish the goal. Summer Place is a perennially mellow, dimly lit joint with an enormous TV in one corner, a handful of half-comfy chairs, a gas-burning fireplace, and various decorations done on par with your average apartment dweller's skills. Like your building lobby, you may also find posted flyers of cars for sale or some other neighborhoody offer on the wall behind the bar.

The drinks are cheap, which is good, and honestly poured, which is better. On busier nights, actors from Union Square theater productions drop in for pre- or postshow cocktails, and hotel district out-of-towners mix it up with neighborhood folks. On slow nights, the atmosphere can be downright discouraging, offering owner/bartender Suzy the opportunity to give herself over completely to her video solitaire addiction. On nights such as these, it's a wise idea to venture in either direction along Bush Street for a livelier atmosphere, unless it's solitude you seek.

Dive rating: ●●●●●●

Yong San Lounge

895 Bush St. (at Taylor St.)
415-771-8138

Muni: 2, 3, 4, 27; Powell cable cars

My traveling buddy Krump walked into this place, took one look around, and said, "This place has the feel of a Thai girly bar, doesn't it? Except it has walls." With its cheap décor à la Orient, ceiling-strung colored Christmas lights, a gorgeous bar lass, and slightly overpriced cocktails, Yong San bears a certain resemblance to those bar/restaurants in a far-away corner of Thailand that Krump and I visited years ago. There, you could tell the menu by the strings of lights that were hung from the rafters: no lights meant Muslim-owned, food only; white lights meant you could get a beer or some whisky with your dinner; colored lights meant a meal, a drink, and after-hours entertainment could be arranged.

I'm not trying to make any point about Yong San, only that it reminded us both of someplace else. In fact, it seemed to me that Bosa, the beautiful bartender, was playing an entirely different game, which required another set of lights altogether. The only rule to this game is that the shortest route between a man and his wallet is a little conversation and a flirty smile. And Yong San's crowd of listless, middle-aged men makes the perfect quarry. The only downside of such a game is that you actually have to hear sad suckers say things like, "You're the apple of my eye" as they hand over singles for more bad Chinese pop on the jukebox.

If you just want to drink and shoot the shit, Bosa's more than happy to regale with tales of Mongolia, Genghis Khan and his enormous empire, horse milk liquor (it's good for you), or the Hollywood celebs known by all worldly Mongols (Richard Gere: he's a Buddhist; Julia Roberts: she visited, etc.). The regulars are a bit tougher to break into, but if you're willing to wait through a handful of $6 Beam and Cokes, you might just get somewhere. If not, when in Rome. . . . Order another drink, come up with some corny lines for the bartender, and hand over a few singles for some romantic ballads in a language you can't understand.

Dive rating: ●●●●●●●

RICHMOND

The Hearth

Muni: 2, 28, 38, 44

The aging neon outside the door has long been a beacon for wayward Irishmen in need of a Richmond District warm-up. But there's no fireplace here, just a gaggle of pint-tossing expats and their friends. Far more low-key than some of the other pubs along Geary's Emerald Alley, the Hearth is blessed with joyful drinkers and a jukebox that most bars would envy. In fact, it's so thick with funk and old-school R&B that it's hard to believe nobody has pried his ass off the barstool to dance on the pool table.

It's mostly thirtysomething fellas at night, but the occasional oldster will pop in for a reasonably priced drink. There are a few micros on tap and a definitive list of bottled favorites. While some of the Irish character seems to have been washed away, it's still a fine enough place to pull down a pint and get in a friendly game of darts or pool. Don't worry, you shouldn't have to wait in line for either one.

Dive rating:

McKenzie's Bar

5320 Geary Blvd. (at 17th Ave.)
415-379-6814

Muni: 2, 28, 38

Here's what's good about McKenzie's: The doors open at 6 a.m., the bar's crowded and lively at 3 p.m. on a Wednesday afternoon, Pabst Blue Ribbon on tap, a bartender who goes by the moniker "Cowboy," a gas fireplace that burns eternally, and a sit-down tabletop-style Ms. Pac-Man in the upstairs mini-lounge — where one might engage in illegal activities, if one were inclined to ignore the sign warning those who sell or do illegal substances that they will face the full wrath of the San Francisco Police Department.

Here's what's bad about McKenzie's: Cheap wine cellar décor items are a terrible match for the wanna-be Scottish pub, hardwood floor leftovers have been given a second life as wood paneling (be careful of splinters if you're a wall-leaner), and the talkative crowd doesn't easily take to strangers.

While the glowing red sign above the door beckons even before the sun has risen, and the bar's namesake clan motto "Luceo Non Uro" (I shine, not burn) may have you thinking you're stepping into a true-blood Scottish bar, McKenzie's is actually a tame gay bar catering to the immediate neighborhood. Don't expect any pretty boys or gym queens here; you're more likely to find odd-earringed, funny hat-wearing middle-aged eccentrics and lifelong San Francisco residents. It's a decent place to while away a lost afternoon in the Richmond, but it's clear that this bar isn't used to strangers wandering in off the street. All the way out at 17th Street and Geary, it's also a bit of a trek except for the determined dive hound. Even so, you'll still find some of the patrons are decent enough to buy you a beer if you beat 'em at pool.

The upstairs lounge is a curious treat — totally separated from the rest of the bar, only offering enough space for half a dozen or so people — with pinball and Ms. Pac-Man.

Dive rating:

Pat O'Shea's Mad Hatter

3848 Geary Blvd. (at 2nd Ave.)
415-752-3148

Muni: 2, 33, 38

Yet another bar with a serious case of schizophrenia, the Mad Hatter lures them in with the motto "We Cheat Tourists & Drunks." If that ain't the perfect invitation, I'm not sure what is. One of many Irish places on Geary's Guinness strip, the Mad Hatter doesn't have the genuine appeal of, say, Ireland's 32 just down the block. But the drinks are cheaper, and they won't charge you three dollars to hear crappy music.

Both an Irish pub and a sports bar, the Mad Hatter is hardly a true dive, but it's a fair enough approximation of one, with its ragged paint and crooked pool table. It is a fine enough bar in the afternoon hours, with two-for-one pitchers during happy hour. Those who shy away from sports or television may want to steer clear, however, as there are a couple dozen TVs in the place, and you pretty much can't look anywhere without getting sucked into a game.

Drop in past 11 at night, however, and you're in for an entirely different vibe. Within a cat's whisker of USF, this seems to be the favored bar of the school's most obnoxious enrollees. The first wave of youngsters to come in each night prompts the exodus of any remaining grizzled drunks at the bar, and then, if you're over age 25, prepare to feel old as the cavernous space fills to capacity and the juvenile collegiate fun begins.

Dive rating:

Trad'r Sam

6150 Geary Blvd. (at 25th Ave.)
415-221-0773

Muni: 2, 29, 38

Constructed as a cheap imitation during Trader Vic's reign as tiki bar king, Trad'r Sam has outlived its inspiration — at least in San Francisco — by several years. That's a bonus for outer Richmond residents with a fondness for faux-Polynesian kitsch, garish decorations, and halfway decent fruit juice and ice cream drinks. Bar crawlers will recognize the tiny U-shaped space by the bright neon sign, with a yellow arrow pointing to the door.

Aside for steady growth in the number of head-shaped sailor mugs and other garage sale finds above the bar, it appears little has changed in Trad'r Sam's sixty-odd-year history. The wicker-constructed "booths," with tropical destinations written above them (Samoa, Tahiti, Hawaii, Guam) are frayed, dirty, and as comfortable as a cushion-deficient couch. On a slow night, you can still get a sense of the failed dreams that once withered and died at the bar here. But this place is now clearly a favorite of University of San Francisco students, so the collegiate vibe, candy pop-loaded jukebox, and drunken kiddy fun can be a bit overwhelming on busy nights. Don't even think about coming on a weekend, and plan your visit in the afternoon or during a school holiday break.

If you manage to find yourself a barstool, peruse the drink menu's twenty-five or so offerings for tropical standards and some only-at-Trad'r-Sam concoctions (keep in mind, this doesn't mean they're good). Don't expect to find out what's inside from the menu; all you'll get are silly descriptions with creative spelling (Chocolate Banana: even the *monkeyes* like this one). There are usually a handful of specials for adventurous souls. At $5 to $20 apiece, the tropical drinks should taste like the tiki gods' nectar . . . but they at least pack a wallop in a hangover-guaranteeing pretty package. Cautious tipplers can still order garden-variety drinks and bottled beer.

Dive rating:

Would You Believe? Cocktails

4562 Geary Blvd.
(at 10th Ave.)
415-452-7444

Muni: 2, 28, 38, 44

In a neighborhood with dozens of other oddly named institutions (My Tofu House, Five Happiness Restaurant, and the prize-winning U.S. Treatment of Difficult & Compliaed [sic] Illness Center), a name like Would You Believe? Cocktails isn't entirely out of place. Once you stop wondering what it is you're being asked to believe, it turns out this is a plain old dive with a Richmond twist.

Centered along Geary's string of Irish bars, Would You Believe? caters to young Asian drinkers from the neighborhood, offering bar snacks of the shrimp chip and shredded squid variety. Even so, the bar attracts a mixed crowd of grizzled old-timers, young couples, solitary TV watchers, and married men drowning their relationship woes. Around holiday time, Halloween or Christmas decorations engage in a raucous competition with standard beer posters and 49ers flags.

Drinks are cheap and honestly poured. Prices are written across the booze bottle labels, making decisions easy for those who can still see across the bar. Feel free to order an unusual cocktail (Mexi-Me Crazy, the Godfather, Leisure Suit, Dragon Slayer, Jackass, House of Cards) from one of the many posted drink menus. But don't expect every bartender to oblige. The fill-in man who is short one voice box hand-signaled his reluctance to poison his clientele with such swill (but, fortunately, didn't hold back on garden-variety cocktails). Once she had taken charge, the owner obliged us with all the frou-frou drinks we could down.

While pool and pinball might are worthy additions to any bar, Would You Believe? offers one innovation entirely its own: railings around the bar. Ostensibly to keep patrons from falling off the raised level of the bar, these rails make it rather easy to belly up for another slug even when walking is a challenge. Would you believe nobody's thought of that yet?

Dive rating:

SOMA

Annie's Cocktail Lounge

15 Boardman Place
(at Bryant St.)
415-703-0865

Muni: 10, 19, 27, 47

Located in the shadow of 850 Bryant (home to county lockup, criminal courts, the district attorney, and seemingly half of San Francisco's off-duty cops), Annie's is like a halfway house for punks who are in need of their first drink after thirty days in the hole. Fans of truly low-budget shit-houses may be disappointed, but if you're looking for a low-key place to sauce your punk ass, this is as fine as you'll find. Run by, you guessed it, Annie, a redheaded punk princess who's almost always behind the bar, making pleasant chitchat and smiling in that way only she can, the place has managed to withstand the ravages of the dot-com era without going out of business or becoming some kind of geek chic hell.

The art-trash-dinosaur-horror movies constantly blaring from the TV are a far cry from standard-issue trash dive TV, and the kitsch potential is high: black velvet paintings, an honorary eight-track player behind the bar, ceramic flamingos, Johnny Depp-obsessed figurines from *Edward Scissorhands* and *Sleepy Hollow*. Local airwaves celeb Terrible Ted, one of KUSF's most loved DJs, has spent a blitz of evenings demonstrating his vocal talent at the twice-weekly DIY karaoke nights (Tuesday and Saturday). Rumor has it that members of legendary California punk progenitors X hang out here when they're visiting from L.A. Otherwise, it's you, Annie, a handful of bike messengers and other rough-around-the-edges types.

In wealthier times, Annie's was a packed place beloved by the swing crowd (where have you gone, daddy-o?). It was damn near impossible to get a cue in edgewise in the tucked-away pool room, and a quiet night was rare. These days, things have mellowed, the crowd has thinned out, and a softer vibe prevails.

Dive rating:

Cassidy's

1145 Folsom St. (between 7th & 8th Sts.)
415-241-9990

Muni: 12, 14, 19, 26

My friend Greg brought me here years ago when I was conducting an experiment in sleeplessness and alcoholic excess, trying to determine if it were possible to make it to work five days a week if you went out seven nights a week. So, it was no surprise that when I returned to Cassidy's recently, I thought I had never been there before, and recalled the place only when I sat down with a Guinness and noticed a cute bike messenger lady twirling to Hank Williams with a shot of whisky in her grip.

A long U-shaped bar with two busy pool tables, $4 pints (ouch), and tons of fine-looking folks who certainly didn't walk out of a J.Crew catalogue, Cassidy's is a scruffy little Irish pub that doesn't draw many real Irishmen. With its deep red walls, the place has the feel of an oversize living room, and that's what I imagine it is for the scads of biker messengers and other two-wheel roughnecks who call this place a second home. It's set up so that everybody's got a view of everybody else, a fact that's not lost on the cliques of single women and men who come here to peruse the offerings and make a stab at going home with more than tomorrow's hangover. Cassidy's is smack in the middle of about two dozen other nightspots in SoMa, so if you're looking for low-key spot to start or end your night, meet up with friends, or try to make some new ones, Cassidy's is the place to do it.

The main draw is the stellar jukebox. It's packed with old punk, metal, random offshoots, country, and much more: Germs, X, Pixies, Ween, Johnny Cash, Black Sabbath . . . you get the picture. It's a requisite stroll down musical memory lane, but don't expect to hear anything you've put on. Everybody's got the same idea, and what's playing right now is from a dollar somebody shoved in last year.

Dive rating:

Dave's

29 3rd St. (at Market St.)
415-495-6726

Muni: 9, 14, 15, 30, 45; Market St. buses and trains
Montgomery St. BART station

Due to the scarcity of bars in the general vicinity of this end of Market Street, you're likely to come across a fairly boisterous crowd at Dave's about an hour after everyone gets off work in the evening. And about an hour after that, most folks will be too drunk to talk — which is exactly how I like my Financial District pals after a long day at the office. Daily drink specials make it easy to drink on the cheap, and cheap bar food — Dave's is also about the only place to get anything to eat in this neighborhood after 7 p.m. — makes it easy to stay here until they make you leave.

Cheap, as I mentioned before, may be the defining element. There's a cheap Formica counter to rest your drink on, the cheap imitation of an old wood bar to look at, cheap local art hanging on the walls, even cheap mirrors to see your cheap reflection in. But hey, cheap is what we like, and cheap is why we're here, and since this is the only game in this corner of town, we'll take it. Ever since the beloved, world-famous 7-11 Club closed down, Dave's has been about the only place to get a cheap drink anywhere downtown.

One other thing I love about Dave's is the Leave a Drink board. The idea is simple: You buy a drink for your buddy on your way out. And when your buddy gets there, it's waiting for him. Doesn't matter when he shows up, or if he shows up, the drink will be there until he drinks it. Tell your local bartender: We should all be so lucky as to have bars with a Leave a Drink board, and buddies who leave us a drink.

Dive rating:

Eagle's Drift-In

527 Bryant St. (at 3rd St.)
415-495-4527

Muni: 10, 12, 15, 30, 45, 47

The SoMa sister to a Sunset District darts hangout, Eagle's is the place you wish you lived upstairs from if you had to live above a bar, as it is a depressingly empty, cavernous place with great bartenders and customers you can usually count on part of one hand. And, unlike practically any other bar in the city, Eagle's is closed on weekends. So, if you lived above Eagle's, you wouldn't have to worry much about your quiet night at home being ruined.

The atmosphere is somewhere out of 1970s-era San Francisco, and the drink prices are too. It also bears the honor of being the best-named bar I've ever come across — apparently a name so good it deserves two bars. In the back room past the pool table are a handful of black Naugahyde booths perfect for cozying up with a group of friends. (Don't worry, you won't have any trouble getting one.) Ditto for getting a game of pool or space at the dartboard. (Real dart buffs and champions ought to head to the other Eagle's for tournaments and dart-related shit-talking.) Want to practice some of your old piano tunes? Step right up, the dusty piano's all yours. Seats aplenty await you at the bar, so take your pick.

Once a venue for local music, it turned into a quirky, sometimes happening spot during the dot-com boom. These days, Eagle's seems to be on its way out. Jane, our bartender, said there was some talk of shutting down on Monday and Tuesday nights too. Our advice to those who can't rest until they've spilled a drink at every bar in town: put an Eagle's notch in your belt soon. It's not waiting around for you to show up.

Dive rating:

Eagle's Drift-In

Red's Java House

Pier 30-32
(The Embarcadero at Bryant St.)
415-777-5626

Muni: N, 12

OK, it's not a bar, but you can get a beer here, and besides, Red's is a San Francisco institution from a storied time that most residents know nothing about. A burger-and-beer joint for generations of longshoremen and other waterfront folks, Red's still carries the no-frills menu and cheap prices that have lured the hungry and thirsty for decades. A trip here is well worth the effort, and the waterfront views from just beneath the Bay Bridge are some of the most awe-inspiring in town.

Now that the very nature of dock work has changed (you can see the container ships steaming into Oakland from here), Red's has seen its clientele shift from burly dockworkers to suit-wearing and khaki-clad downtowners. You will still occasionally run into working-class folks, particularly at the noon hour during the week. But Red's, like the city it calls home, is forever changed. This change has prompted a remodeling, a price hike, and a few heavily debated additions like a french fryer.

It's perhaps best not to worry about what's different. What's worth making the trip here is what's still the same: cheap burgers (always a minute past well done), strong coffee, and cold longnecks you can bring outside for a view of the bay. Take a walk from here and you really can imagine a different city of San Francisco from a long time ago.

Dive rating:

SAN FRANCISCO'S BEST DIVE BARS

Rich's Club 93

93 9th St. (at Mission St.)
415-621-6183

Muni: 14, 19, 26; Market St. buses and trains
Civic Center BART station

In a blasted-out section of skid row — the requisite boarded-up corner store, a burned-out SRO hotel down the street, rambling drunks wandering down dark and empty alleys — Rich's is an oasis. Sure it's an oasis because it is the only bar for blocks, but the place is also cleaner and homier than you would have expected. In other words, it's cleaner than it needs to be, at least in the world of dive bars.

Rich's does have its cast of characters from the neighborhood: the faded blonde beauty queen of a bartender, the grizzled old-timer who crutches himself out to the sidewalk to smoke at ten-minute intervals, the sixty-year-old boozer who never has to order a drink because of his universally understood nod, the trivia-addicted overweight woman who guards her machine. But it's also a bar where, if you stumble in with three friends on a Saturday night, the place is all yours. There's two pool tables, two Triple Play machines, free popcorn and Goldfish (did someone say dinner?), darts, a foosball machine, and a jukebox filled with old soul and R&B.

Those who don't want to pick their way through the tap selection should make a beeline for PBR on draft, but the mixed drinks are cheap and strong. On Sunday nights, regulars drop in for a double-elimination pool tournament with a cash prize for the top three players. Most other nights, it's you, a few regulars, and some slow music to put your mind at ease. But please remember, there's no sleeping at the bar.

Dive rating:

SUNSET/ WEST PORTAL/ PARKSIDE

Grandma's Saloon

In one of those curious geographical oxymorons that only a real-estate wizard could have cooked up, San Francisco's foggiest neighborhood became known as the Sunset. The sand dunes were paved over and the neighborhood acquired a post-WWII veneer that exists to the present day. Add to that several decades of demographic shift and you've got a neighborhood that's equal parts urban suburb, melting pot, and surreal residential wonderland. Commercial strips like Taraval offer amazing varieties of ethnic eateries, small independent businesses, and treasured neighborhood dives.

An old friend of mine used to drive all the way out to drink at Grandma's, for some untold reason he couldn't explain. He'd stumbled on the place after a summertime concert at Stern Grove and it became the secret little place where everybody knew his name.

Regulars are indeed known by name at Grandma's, but the flip side of that is that newcomers may be greeted with suspicion. On one night I visited, I never was able to shake the bartender's curious, wary glances. Even so, it's a cozy enough little place with a brick wall on one side and cheap wood paneling around the rest of the room. Above the bar are a hundred patches ripped from the sleeves of police and fire department uniforms, a sign of the huge number of cops and firemen who have put down residential roots in the neighborhood.

Newcomers should know that stick is taken very seriously here. Players arrive with their own cues, and sloppy playing isn't tolerated. The resident shark on one Friday night was a fiftyish woman who seemed to be under the control of a wicked speed habit. One slop-mitigating rule that other tables citywide could adopt is the eight-ball kitty: if the cue ball hits the floor, you gotta pay fifty cents into a kitty and whoever sinks the eight ball on a break wins the pot.

Dive rating: ●●●●●●●

Miraloma Club

Just when you thought there were no strip malls in San Francisco, along comes a strip mall bar in one of the most historic strip malls you'll ever find — not that it looks much different from any strip mall in America. Inside this longstanding Twin Peaks establishment, you'll see a 1940s-era photo of the recently built neighborhood, and lo and behold, there's the Miraloma Club, beckoning automotive alcoholics as it still does today with its beaming neon sign.

The crowd is young, neither too hip nor too boring, attractive but not gorgeous — lots of local folks who suck back shots with abandon. Embedded in either corner of the bar is an enormous big-screen TV, perennially tuned to ESPN or Fox Sports. Pool sharks hustle it at a table in the back room. Drinks are mixed strong enough even for folks who maintain a permanent blood-alcohol level. With more than a dozen beers on tap — not all of them overflavored microbrews — there's plenty to please even the shot-phobic.

It's a tough place to get to if you don't live in the immediate neighborhood, but it's a worthy stopover after a sightseeing trip to Twin Peaks or Mount Davidson. Like any decent strip mall, there's a huge parking lot.

Dive rating: ●●●●●

The Old Rogue

A fond farewell to the Deuces, a longtime Parkside standby for 6 a.m. boozing and off-sale purchase. It's now the Old Rogue, a regrettable name if I've ever heard one, and sunrise drinkers now have to wait until eight for a shot of Irish whisky and a Bud Light. Not much else has changed though; the Irish brogue is just as thick, Guinness is still poured, a gray haze hangs in the air, and the place sticks to the old tradition of live music from local bands on most weekends. There's sometimes a $2 special on some bottled beer for weekend events, offsetting the cover for music, if there is one.

With décor straight out of <I>Western PreFab Living,<P> the Old Rogue musters the feel of an old-time saloon built in 1988. The wood paneling, California ranch home cabinetry, a corner devoted to motorcycle photos, and assorted cowboy-bar-meets-Dublin tchotchkes muster a feel you'd be hard-pressed to find anywhere else in the city (or want to find anywhere else in the city).

A large part of the clientele hails from the Emerald Isle, and a fair number of these fellas are dart players. Darts, in fact, seems to be the main event on many a weeknight, when two of the three TVs are dim and the assorted drinkers watch each toss with rapt attention (proving once again that folks, deprived of television, will watch just about anything for entertainment). Beyond that, there's pool, lots of beer on tap, and enough Aerosmith on the juke to send a dozen Irishmen into occasional spasms of air guitar.

Dive rating: ●●●●

Portals Tavern

179 West Portal Ave.
(between 14th Ave. & Vicente St.)
415-731-1208

Muni: K, L, M, 17, 48

I'll be the first to admit that there is little reason beyond amnesia to venture all the way out to West Portal to go drinking. For those who haven't wandered the city's farthest western districts, the surreal scenery of this not-of-the-modern-era neighborhood may literally drive one to drink, and then some. That said, if you happen to find yourself in these parts and in need of refreshment, Portals is a fine place to imbibe.

A true neighborhood bar drawing neighborhood people, Portals conjures the feeling of a cozy bomb shelter, whether you're drinking at 1 p.m. or 1 a.m. The wooden beams overhead, the brick floors underfoot and the thick wood planks on the walls create a warm atmosphere, drawing the locals 'round the semicircular bar. Since it's an establishment that caters largely to regulars, people know each other and tend to feel fairly comfortable getting completely no-holds-barred ploughed. The last time we visited, a drunken marital spat over the trivia machine was resolved with that small-town standby, a quick hush and shaming glances from all. The offending husband was cut off from additional quarters — having already lost his drinking permit — but escaped the ego-crushing 86. When ABBA came on the jukebox, he slowly began to dance, then shuffled over to say how much he and the old ball and chain loved *Mamma Mia!*, the recent musical based on the music of the Swedish supergroup.

Cocktails are strong, and there's a short but adequate selection of beers on tap, both micro and macro. The bartenders are friendly enough to indulge wagerly patrons in games of liar's dice. On game nights, the Portals transforms from a fading Irish institution to full-on sports bar. True to its sport spirit, the place has also organized a handful of city-league sports teams, whose trophies occupy their own shelf opposite the bar.

There are also a few nice surprises at Portals, most notably the sit-down Ms. Pac-Man and a small patio for those who alternately crave fresh air or cigarettes.

Dive rating: ●●●●●●

Sand Bar

3639 Taraval St. (at 46th Ave.)
415-759-7263

Muni: L, 18, 48

Don't let the 1980s retro sign fool you. There's nothing cheesy about this almost beachfront bar. Drawing post-ride surfers, young homeowners, and the usual cast of divegoers, the Sand Bar is neighborhood drinking at its best. It's also a couple blocks from the zoo, so if some family member ever drags you out there and you just can't stand the idea of watching those depressed penguins anymore, take a load off at the only diamond-shaped bar you'll ever visit. That's right — diamond! This town's got circular, square, L-shaped, and other odd formations on which to lean an elbow, but Sand's is pure parallelogram. Finally, somebody made something of ninth-grade geometry.

Sand's is the kind of place you'd be grateful to find after the fog's rolled in on your day at the beach. The regulars are talkative to outsiders, and the drinks are cheap and strong enough for you to want to stick around for a while. The jukebox is loaded with the usual rock anthems: AC/DC, Boston, Billy Idol, Stones, and more Beatles than you can stand to hear in one night. Be forewarned that Boston may set some of the old-timers into odd little shuffles, even if they are too drunk to walk to the bathroom on two bum legs. The place is also dog friendly, and there's always a fire going in the fireplace to warm your post-ocean chills.

On game days, there's sometimes a pot of soup or something else to put in your belly besides booze. On an evening visit, the crock-pot was still cranking at 11 p.m., even as the bartender warned those with taste buds away from the daily special. Be forewarned that game days may be canceled in the event the bar hasn't paid its cable bill, which has happened at least once in recent memory.

Dive rating: ●●●●●●

Shannon Arms

915 Taraval St. (at 19th Ave.)
415-665-1223

Muni: L, 28

A visit to the Shannon Arms may serve as a reminder of the socially dysfunctional nature of the average American dive, where conversation flags because the oftenest way to drink is alone. While we may be attached to our own particular approach to the drinking establishment, it's nice to see that in other parts of the world, bars can be something entirely different.

Once inside these double doors, you get the feeling you've stepped into a real Dublin pub, not an Americanized version called The Irish Pub. Signs in Irish dangle from above, painted slats identify this hallowed ground as Eire, a thick haze clings in the air, and the bellowing volume of a hundred lilting voices deafens the ears. But a quick glance around the room reveals few raised pints of Harp, Smithwick's, Guinness, or Beamish; this crowd is decidedly in the grips of Budweiser, Coors, and MGD.

Large numbers of Irish expats call the Sunset home, and this bar is certainly one of the community focal points, a crowded, boisterous meeting place for all who hail from the Emerald Isle. While most folks tend to gather at the bar, there are tables along the opposite wall that draw those seeking alone time, and an amateur-friendly pool table in the back room.

Though primarily a bar for men in their twenties, weekend nights attract graying couples, groups of friends, a handful of women, and one or two old-timers. The banter is loud and nonstop, as is the drinking. While it's clearly a happening place if you're Irish, the community may seem a bit tough to break into. But surely that's nothing a few drinks can't remedy.

Dive rating: ⚫⚫⚫⚫⚫

Silver Spur

1914 Irving St. (at 20th Ave.)
415-564-4250

Muni: N, 28, 29, 71

"Most people wouldn't even put that up in their closet," one patron said to me as I looked at a framed photomontage of the worst bachelor party in history. There she was in all her bare beaver and small-breasted glory, surrounded by a half dozen shirtless beer bellies. It's really the deterrent any uncertain husband needs — especially if somebody's got a camera — for the self-humiliation he will have to put himself through before signing any permanent legal documents. At any rate, said photo gallery serves as the best piece of interior décor the Silver Spur has to offer.

Hardly a choice watering spot, but a watering spot nonetheless, the Spur is not without its charms, many of them in a friendly-local-of-the-Inner-Sunset sort of way. An alcoholic oasis among a desert of cheap Asian restaurants and junk shops along Irving, the Spur has all the basic amenities: blaring TVs, a pool table, a metal-stocked jukebox, and cheap-ass drinks. Primarily a haunt of locals, it seems everybody knows each other fairly well, and the bartender, Joe, keeps things fairly chummy. Don't expect everybody to warm up, but by the time you've ordered a second or third drink, you might just have made a bunch of new friends. Patrons range from twentysomething to older than the hills — all of them sharing one of the finest human traits: the love of hard drinking.

On a recent visit, I noticed the bar's owners had decided to circumvent California law and install a number of Altoids-tin ashtrays for customers so inclined. We predict that by the time this book is printed, said benefit to nicotine addicts will be no longer.

Dive rating: ●●●●●●●

TK's

328 West Portal Ave. (at 14th Ave.)
415-566-9444

Muni: K, M, 17, 48

The glowing red neon will be your guide, whether it's midnight or 6 a.m., as TK's is another one of those alcoholic Shangri-las built for early morning inebriation. A comfy little rail of a bar, with seats for twelve and not much else, TK's has a mellow 1970s feel, with a well-worn Formica-topped bar, cheap wood siding, a curious Ford administration style cubbyhole ceiling pattern, and a gallery of boxing photos to keep your eyes occupied.

True to the vast western stretches of the city, darts is the rule here, with frequent tournaments and a gallery of plaques and trophies in a stairway. (If you're not a champ, steer clear, as you'll be out of your league here.) There's no pool table, and only pinball, video golf, and trivia games by way of non-drinking entertainment. But the beer is cheap and the jukebox is passable. The place is dominated by a tight-knit crew of locals — a tough crowd to crack for outsiders. Said locals also tend to keep up a steady bitch session about whichever of their friends just stepped out to smoke or haven't yet made it to the bar that night, so if you want to know all about people you don't know, just stare down into your drink and listen quietly.

Dive rating: ●●●●●●

TENDERLOIN

TENDERLOIN SPECIAL: GOOD COP, BAD COP

World travelers and former GIs who spent time in Asia will recognize a familiar and lucrative tag-team form of bartending in many of the Tenderloin's bars. It's a familiar setup involving two female bartenders — oftentimes Korean, but not always — and some lonely old (and young) fellas.

The setup is as follows: The younger and/or cuter bartender flirts with the patrons, encourages them to buy her drinks or give her a couple bucks for the jukebox, and generally assists even the most determined misanthrope in having a bit of fun. She can get quite drunk and lively over the course of matching shots and pouring drinks. And so can you.

Just when you think that she's drunk enough to have forgotten the last round or two, the other bartender swoops in from the other end of the bar, where she's been idly watching TV or talking on the phone — but keeping a sober and accurate tab on what you've been drinking, and just as importantly, all the shots you may have bought for your new bartender/drinking pal when you thought nobody was paying attention. So, if you're drinking in the Tenderloin and the hot, young bartender seems a little too attentive, my advice is, keep your wits and you may just hold onto your money long enough to buy yourself another round.

The Brown Jug

496 Eddy St. (at Hyde St.)
415-441-8404

Muni: 19, 27, 31, 38

In San Francisco's best neighborhood for cut-rate boozing, the Brown Jug is king. You might snicker at the would-be Barbary Coast décor, the Victorian wallpaper, the yellowed posters framed and tacked to the walls, and the antique guns nailed behind the bar, but this bar is genuine in one sense: the TL's most authentic characters gather here to tie one on with abandon. After a couple of nights here, you too will become a sworn devotee at this altar of inebriation.

The Jug is the city at its polyglot, multi-culti best: Drunk is spoken in all languages and inflections (although knowing a little Spanish might do you well around the pool table). As a daytime drinking spot, it's not much different from any of the other places in the immediate vicinity (which is to say, it's just fine). But after dark, the regulars come out to play and the Brown Jug begins to shine.

The place attracts all types: gay, straight, transgender, black, white, Latino, male, female, freakish, normal, hipster, unstylish, broke, and well-off. Most patrons are friendly after a drink or two — and some of them are especially friendly, if you give them the chance.

On a particularly sotted night, the neighbor on the next barstool described the horrors of going home alone as he gazed around the hazy room through heavily lidded eyes, undoubtedly searching for a suitable partner. Finding nobody else would talk to him, he struck up slurred conversation and invited me back to his place. After I turned him down in favor of another bottle of Bud, he whispered fantasies of foreskins and more into my ear. At some point, he turned his attention to the half-finished shot in front of him, and after finishing that, stumbled out into the night.

Diving rating: ●●●●●●●

Club 501

501 Jones St. (at O'Farrell St.)

Muni: 2, 3, 4, 27, 38

The simple beauty of "501" numbered in black and a martini glass sandwiched between tandem offerings of "Draft" and "Cocktails" cannot be overstated. This sign on the corner of Geary and Jones is the only indication that you've hit rock-bottom on a seedy stretch of asphalt in the Tenderloin's Curry Alley. At an intersection favored by crackheads, hustlers, and lovers of cheap Pakistani food lives 501, perhaps the diviest spot in the city, a place where the street meets the night in a delicious combination of character and grime.

501's the kind of place where a couple of thugs will walk in every half hour and ask the feisty Chinese bartender if she's seen Devonne, who hasn't shown up on his corner all night. There's also a mysterious back room behind a curtain of love beads that empties out when newcomers arrive. The clientele is a Tenderloin mix of tough gay fellas, Chinese alcoholics, adventurous tourists, wrinkled women who have spent a lifetime of nights in a bar just like this, and weary veterans coming in to take another look at the chorus of Navy caps on the wall behind the bar. At the end of the bar, there's always a perpetually parked old-timer who finished his drink an hour ago, but isn't ready for another, as here's better than home. (Or here may be home.) To top it all off, a crude yet classy nude painting sets the perfect tone for whatever adventure the night has in store.

The first time I came in, after an overwhelming plate of tandoori down at Shalimar, we made small talk with the Indonesian bartender and tilted back an uncountable number of $2.50 Budweisers. On one of the resultant trips to the john, I turned around to find a freshly used condom sitting like a cherry on top of the trash can. These days you need the key to get into the bathroom — a measure undertaken, I'm sure, to quell such unauthorized access (or perhaps to ensure a degree more privacy). There's also the heartwarming note tacked up above the toilet: "Please stand closer to the toilet because your big John is not as long as you think."

The jukebox is loud as hell, and there's plenty of old soul to get you going. Well drinks are cheap (there ain't much in the way of call licks anyway), and the bottled beer is cheaper. PBR occasionally flows from the tap, when the tap occasionally works. Oh, and that foreign king of beers, Lowenbrau, is always cold. C'mon, when was the last time you had a Lowenbrau?

Dive rating: ⚫⚫⚫⚫⚫⚫⚫⚫⚫⚫

Edinburgh Castle

950 Geary St. (at Polk St.)
415-885-4074

Muni: 2, 3, 4, 19, 38, 47, 49

It's not much of a dive, but no dedicated bar crawler should pass his days without at least one sotted night at the Edinburgh, where many a spirits-sipper has been known to slip into a dialect much harder to grasp than Scottish. Big beams of wood define this cavernous space, with a huge main floor, a mid-level pool area, peanut galleries above the main floor on both sides, as well as a tucked-away back room upstairs where generally bad bands and worse poets compete for a pittance of an audience.

While the mystery of where the fish and chips come from has long been solved, they're still a great grease bomb to help soak up the deleterious effects of single-malt scotch and British beer. Order from your waitress and the fish will come wrapped in newspaper 15 minutes later. At $4, the beers aren't cheap (thriftmisers drink Bud), but happy hour specials can make an early evening here easy to stomach. Also, there's never a cover (unless you want to make a small donation to bands bad enough they should be buying you a beer), and the place is utterly unpretentious. Don't worry, most comers will easily find a stool or a booth and move right in among the youngish crowd.

Those who can't stand trivia nights are advised: do not come on Tuesday nights. The pub quiz attracts geeks and drunks from all over the city to compete for enough cash to buy a couple rounds. Local literati also show up for occasional poetry readings, and some high-caliber authors — including Irvine Welsh — have made an appearance or two. The Edinburgh Castle, with its unassuming, dark, and slightly dinging façade, is a San Francisco institution.

Dive rating:

Only in Frisco

C Bobby's Owl Tree
Double Play
Gangway
John Murio's Trophy Room
Li Po
Red's Java House
Rite Spot
Spec's
Tommy's Joynt
Zeitgeist

Gangway

841 Larkin St. (at Geary St.)
415-776-6828

Muni: 2, 3, 4, 19, 38, 47, 49

You'll recognize the Gangway from the prow of a boat sticking out above the doorway along one of Polk Gulch's seedier stretches. Inside, the nautical theme meets cowboy décor, with mirrored portholes cut into the rough wood interior. Primarily a gay bar catering to a mostly middle aged crowd, you'll also find the occasional fag hag, transgender, or mystery guest. The Gangway's open enough for folks of any persuasion, but be forewarned that groups of straight folks aren't exactly common here, so if you stop in among all your hetero friends and lovers, expect to be treated like vacationing foreigners. The Gangway isn't a major pickup joint, but it's a good place for conversation, if you can hear yourselves above the diva-stocked jukebox.

If you're lucky enough to meet the soft-spoken bartender, Johnny Wise, you'll be in for an extraordinary evening of bar tales. A barkeep for nearly forty years, Mr. Wise knows all the regulars, and he's happy enough to point them out to newcomers. Many people, however, come in to drink alone. While chatting with Mr. Wise is always a pleasure, the same is not necessarily the case with every patron in here — a few of whom seem incapable of pleasant chitchat.

Drinks are strong as they should be, and fairly priced. A word to those who can't make up their minds: Don't let Mr. Wise make you his world-famous frothy blender concoction. It's downright dangerous. On the upside, the pool table is frequently deserted.

Dive rating: ●●●●●●

Hanaro

Muni: 2, 3, 4, 19, 38, 47, 49

This is the kind of place where you're likely to hear somebody muttering something incomprehensible under his breath about you as you walk through the door, and again as you leave. Yet another Tenderloin bar catering to old salts on a limited income, Hanaro draws a handful of grumpy middle-agers who wander in to sulk and talk trash with two past-their-prime barmaids. And said barmaids, two aging Korean women who run the place, seem to have spent a lifetime pulling tears and years from drink-laden men, and their bar demeanor at 1 a.m. is somewhere between flirting for one last dollar tip and resignation that tonight's highlight might be closing ten minutes early. Even so, these girls have had a thousand nights like this one and have been at it long enough to be able to dispatch a drunken regular homeward with a single look.

Don't come here looking to be impressed by the decoration, which seems to be the product of a bargain-basement sale on 1970s-era home design: thin cinder-brick walls and mirror tiles on the ceiling and behind the bar. Fresh flowers are always a nice touch at any bar, but here they come wilted just for you. A potpourri basket above the sink in the men's room does little to dispatch the familiar scent of diving's inevitable by-products.

Older Asian men stop in for Budweisers and paper plates of peanuts and seaweed snacks. The jukebox offers bad Asian pop and '70s American cheese rock for your listening pleasure. Probably the best thing about Hanaro is that you won't know anyone when you walk in the door. And you won't when you leave, either.

Dive rating:

Ha-Ra Club

875 Geary St. (at Larkin St.)
415-673-3148

Muni: 2, 3, 4, 19, 38, 47, 49

Nestled among the remnants of Polk Gulch's teen hustling hot spots and the Tenderloin's tranny mecca is one of the city's long-favored dumps, a dive-lover's dream for over half a century and counting. The exterior is bland gone bad, but inside these brick walls you'll find a crooked pool table, an old phone booth that lights up when you shut the door, and a jukebox with some of the worst music from the past thirty years. In other words, a perfect place to blissfully waste a night, or a lifetime.

Back when the neighborhood was a bit dodgier, well-dressed newcomers might have felt a bit out of place among the neighborhood drunks and off-duty dancers from nearby clubs. While there's still a contingent of regulars and oddballs, the Ha-Ra also pulls in a smattering of lost or slumming hipsters, men with "dates," and nightcapping tourists. But it's also a wonderful place to drink sans companion. True to its purpose, the Ha-Ra lives up to the calling of every dive bar near and far: if it weren't for that drink in your hand, you'd be the loneliest person in the world. Speaking of that drink in your hand, don't forget to order a beer here simply for the sheer novelty of sipping Bud or Miller High Life from 7-ounce kid-size bottles. (Where were those when I was a kid?)

Rick, the bar owner, is a pleasant chap who inherited the place from his dad, a former pro boxer whose pictures line the walls. Top among the Ha-Ra's myriad charms is bartender Carl, who's made a long habit of insulting most who walk through his doors. Don't expect to have a reason to leave a tip, as Carl will more than likely ridicule your drink order and 86 anything questionable from the jukebox (he may, in fact, nix any and all music you've paid for if he doesn't like your first poorly picked song). But he's also seen it all over the years, so you're just another shrub he's got to prune a few times before he's gonna let you plant roots around one of his barstools.

Dive rating: ⬤⬤⬤⬤⬤⬤⬤

Ha-Ra Club

Harrington's Harry Pub

460 Larkin St. (at Turk St.)
415-775-1160

Muni: 5, 19, 31

Have you ever walked into a bar that was already closed? That's what the bartender asked me the first time I tried to enter Harrington's. It was about 11 on a weeknight and he was sick of holding court to a crowd of ghosts. He told me that the bar was closed for the night, and that he and his girl would meet us at the Brown Jug a couple blocks away, which he did. But that's another story.

Harrington's is a sleepy Tenderloin hofbrau favored by slumming office workers from Civic Center government buildings by day, and an entirely separate but small coterie of hard-drinking, Bollocks-spouting locals at night. Arranged like a reform school cafeteria, the main part of the bar is just a bunch of crooked tables and cheap chairs laid out on a stone floor. During meal hours, you can pick up decent grit at fair prices, but the real action is at the bar, where a solid wood rail serves to guide the stumbling, and Guinness is only two drunken syllables away.

Harrington's tends to be busiest during weekday happy hour. On weekend nights, it is usually the opposite (not busy). Either way, you'll have no trouble getting a stool at the long bar, and there's plenty of eye candy to look at — a picture of JFK throwing a football, an enormous fish tank on one end, James Brown dolls. The bartenders sometimes speak in an unfathomable brogue, but not to worry, the incomprehension is not a two-way street — they still understand your drink orders.

Dive rating: ●●●●●●

Ride the wire – Cable car bars

C Bobby's Owl Tree
Chelsea Place
Kennedy's
Kimo's
La Rocca's Corner
Route 101
Summer Place
Yong San Lounge

High Tide

High Tide

600 Geary St. (at Jones St.)
415-771-3145

Muni: 2, 3, 4, 27, 38

Let the garish neon sign with its blinking lights be your guide and you'll find yourself inside one of the Tenderloin's true-blue dives. Above the bar — and perhaps the draw for many of the place's single, male inebriants — is a painting of a topless Asian woman, illuminated with gusto by a lamp and a reflector fashioned from aluminum foil.

If the antics of the female bartender aren't enough to occupy your attention (believe me, they should be), there's a single pool table, well-worn and surrounded by a dozen or so crooked cues. An enormous window facing the street means that after dark, passersby may watch your game, or better yet, curse your bad shots or pound the window in anger. The jukebox offers a few gems, but mostly it's standard fare: Elvis, Clapton, Willie Nelson, etc.

Even if you find your bartender pulling shots with the best of them, don't expect to be able to slip away without paying for your drink. She's got a mind like a trap, a drunken trap mind you, but it's still a trap. After last call one night, she was having trouble kicking out the patrons as she tried to close up. After a few rounds of denial ("I'm not drunk"), she eventually admitted what everyone already knew ("I'm fucked up. As usual."). Long live the High Tide.

Dive rating:

Kimo's

1351 Polk St. (at Pine St.)
415-885-4535

Muni: 19, 47, 49; California cable car

I can remember Kimo's for as long as I can remember San Francisco. As a teenager, I would skateboard down to Sardar's Hi-Times in the quest for the perfect bong, always passing a gallery of street-watchers in the huge windows at Kimo's. Before that, I remember my folks rushing us past whatever dangers lay behind Kimo's wide-open door, on our way from some cheap motel to some cheap restaurant. (Cheapness, like bad breath or the love of hard drink, is often inherited.)

The upper end of Polk Gulch is making the transformation from seedy, gay-oriented street scene to vibrant, mainstream urban neighborhood with a gay undercurrent. Restaurants are sprouting up left and right. Bars are closing and reopening as much fancier versions of the shit-holes they once were. Hustlers are moving farther down Polk toward the Civic Center to make a living. But Kimo's remains the area's quintessential gay hangout. For a quarter century, it's been a rendezvous for friends, lonely old-timers, hustlers and those who love them, and these days, an increasing number of plain ol' straight folks.

In recent years, Kimo's has built a reputation as a spot for loud punk music, goth rock, and other underground sounds in its upstairs venue (despite the serious efforts of some determined neighbors to get the music turned off). The music crowd is younger, straighter, and couldn't give two shits about who or what used to define Kimo's, and the spillover is taking its toll on the downstairs bar's longtime feel. Like everything else about San Francisco, it's a place in flux. But some of the old character will never fade — it's still a place where you might step outside to hear a tranny ask her best friend, "C'mon, can't you give a bitch a ride?"

Dive rating: ●●●●●●

Kimo's

Mr. Lee-Ona's Cocktail Lounge

301 Turk St.
(at Leavenworth St.)
415-292-9803

Muni: 5, 19, 31

If most Tenderloin gay bars tend toward the half-empty, Mr. Lee-Ona's goes the other way, toward the overflow. It also goes both ways, as everyone, gay, straight or otherwise, is welcome. It's a pickup scene where nobody cares who or what you pick up. Mr. Lee-Ona's core crowd may be predominantly middle-aged gay guys, but the rest of the large mix is a who's who of who's gay who doesn't hang in the Castro: black men sipping Cosmos, white men drinking beer, septuagenarian Argentines with a predilection for Spanish-language literature, solitary silent types, greasy hippies, eye-patch-wearing baldheads shimmying at the bar, off-night trannies.

The drinks are dangerously strong and deliciously priced. The soundtrack is all camp, all the time, but even this adds to the over-the-top hilarity of the place. If you don't hear Madonna six times an hour, the jukebox must be busted. And if you're under age 40, expect to be carded by the bartender. That said, about ten seconds after you come in the door, you're going to have half a dozen new friends, at least for the night.

You'll almost always see somebody familiar here. The last time I stopped for a cocktail, I ran into the security guard of the building across the street from where I live. Throughout the night, he reminded us again and again that he wasn't gay. "I like ladies. I just like to party. I like to party. Don't matter who I party with. I like ladies." Again and again, all night long. You may not meet the love of your life at Mr. Lee-Ona's, but a short-term sugar daddy certainly isn't out of the question.

Dive rating:

Gay bars

Gangway
Kimo's
McKenzie's
Mr. Lee-Ona's
The Transfer
Trax
Wild Side West (lesbian)

Nite Cap

699 O'Farrell St. (at Hyde St.)
415-776-5711

Muni: 2, 3, 4, 19, 27, 38

The Night Cap may be the Tenderloin's friendliest place to juice up, and it's not just because the world is a beautiful place at $2.50 per drink. Like many of its neighboring sauce-spots, this bar suffers from a bit of a split personality disorder between its old-school cadre of mellow daytime drinkers and a younger, working-class nighttime crowd. But regardless of the hour, the bartenders are a pleasant bunch, and some of the patrons are so starved for conversation they'll continue talking to themselves if you wander off. On a recent visit, a regular impressed half the bar with the high scores he received on some computer-tech test that was soon to be his key to gainful employment — if only he could drag himself out of the bar to look for work.

A super low-key vibe permeates the tiny place, and despite its rough-and-tumble location, it's far from sketchy. Don't come here looking for excitement, but if it's a shot and a beer and a game of pool you're after, this is the perfect place. Most of the time, you'll find after-work folks and lonely souls looking for a game to watch or a glass to stare into. The jukebox is run-of-the-mill: Kiss, Patsy Cline, the Stones, the Who, Blondie, Devo. Basically, the Night Cap is a fine place to end up when your highest expectation is leaving the apartment.

Dive rating: ● ● ● ● ● ●

Route 101

1332 Van Ness Ave. (at Bush St.)
415-673-9044

Muni: 2, 3, 4, 19, 47, 49; California cable car

Perhaps most useful for helping lost tourists navigate their way to the Golden Gate Bridge on the sign-deficient stretch of Van Ness that doubles as 101, this lackluster dive is a popular drinking slum for the well-heeled citizens of Russian Hill, Pacific Heights, and other nearby upscale neighborhoods. If one were to believe the mural back by the pool table, Route 101 is San Francisco's version of Cheers. It's true, quite a few people know each other's names, but unless you're waiting for a flick to begin or an afternoon downpour to subside, you will find little reason to stick around long enough to learn any of them.

While the management has cut traditional corners in decoration and bathroom upkeep, it's clear some profits have been sunk into one accoutrement not typically found at your average dive: an enormous flat-screen television, surrounded by its own pod of couches. However, due to the odd layout of this cavernous place, nobody but those sitting on said couches can get a glimpse of the thing.

The two pool tables in the back are a big draw, and the low-key atmosphere is far from unpleasant, especially compared with nearby Polk Street, which continues to evolve as a destination for the affluent and beautiful. Don't expect wonders from the run-of-the-mill jukebox. A table in the front window offers a perfect vantage point for people-watching and catching the action on Van Ness. Be forewarned, however, that it also allows envious drunks and street urchins a perfect view of your good times.

Dive rating: ●●●●●●

TENDERLOIN

SAN FRANCISCO'S BEST DIVE BARS

Tommy's Joynt

1101 Geary Blvd. (at Van Ness Ave.)
415-775-4216

Muni: 2, 3, 4, 19, 38, 47, 49

Though not strictly a bar, Tommy's is a San Francisco institution — one of the few places you can get a decent meal at midnight, not to mention a fine place to grab a beer at any hour. There's usually a line at the door, as the crowd assembles at the counter to order pasta, meatloaf, prime rib, buffalo stew, soups, and other hearty supper fare. While it ain't the city's culinary finest, it's fine enough, particularly if you've lost your strength midway through a Tenderloin bar crawl. Prices are fair ($4 to $8 for most everything) and portions are generous. Those who feel shortchanged can shore up the difference by making a run at the pot of free pickles past the cash register.

Patrons range from sports buffs to homeless folks to urban freaks, plus the occasional mecca-seeking metalheads paying tribute. (Tommy's was a favorite spot for members of Metallica and the place where former bassist Jason Newsted was asked to join the band.)

Most people stop in to eat, but there's a fine bar for drinking and several TVs for whichever games are on. Take a gander at the extensive international beer list. They usually are out of the more obscure offerings, but if you've been craving that beer you once had in Poland or Peru, this is the place you're likely to find it.

Artifacts from a long-gone San Francisco line the wall, and the décor is most garish. The best time to visit Tommy's is in the wee hours, when nothing really matters besides filling one's belly enough to be able to journey on to the next bar.

Dive rating: ●●●●●●

Tommy's Joynt

XS

662 Polk St. (at Eddy St.)
415-771-8063

Muni: 19, 31, 38, 47, 49

You'll recognize it by the marquee outside that advertises the Wooden Horse, the gay bar that formerly occupied this tiny half of a hole-in-the-wall. Located in Polk's tranny hooker ground zero, XS is an itsy-bitsy haven for punk rock. The walls are adorned with concert posters, everything from the Butthole Surfers to Incredibly Strange Wrestling. The curved wooden bar beckons you to order another, with PBR being a clear favorite, and be sure to take in the collection of choice bumper stickers. ("I _ Mormon Pussy" wins, with "I'm just a social drinker, but I smoke crack like a motherfucker" pulling a close second.)

The clientele is an odd mix of Wooden Horse holdovers and wandering pubcrawlers. Its prime Civic Center location hasn't been lost on off-duty bike messengers, and you'll notice a hundred or so ripped-off nametags from California Culinary Academy graduates, as the school is right across the street. You can usually find a stool, and given the small crowds, it's easy to imagine that you own the place. Even so, XS is so tiny that a handful of people off the street will tip the bar into overflow. All in all, it's an amiable crowd — the place is simply too small for it not to be.

Dive rating: ●●●●●●

THE BEST DIVE BARS IN THE BAY AREA, OUTSIDE OF SAN FRANCISCO

EAST BAY

The Alley   3325 Grand Ave., Oakland, 510-444-8505

Some call it a firetrap; others a rat trap. Either way, this Oakland institution hasn't changed in more than 50 years, aside from the steady addition of business cards to its well-coated walls. But the drinks are cheap, and Rod the piano player is a legend.

Bigum's Silver Lion   4901 Telegraph Ave., Oakland, 510-653-0921

Oakland's most interestingly named hideaway for daytime drunks. It's dark, cavernous, and boasts an assortment of skull-inspired artwork on the walls.

The Graduate
6202 Claremont Ave., Oakland, 510-655-8847

Don't be fooled by the name: If there are any Cal folks in here, they've long since sauced their smarts on the high-octane cocktails. A dingy neighborhood haunt, with its own cadre of regulars, the Graduate is a fine place to spend an afternoon and get to know somebody on a barstool near you.

Hotsy Totsy Club   601 San Pablo Ave., Albany, 510-525-9964

The Hotsy Totsy is worth a visit based on the strength of its name alone. It is, however, worth a visit otherwise too. Low key, with fortified drinks, pool, shuffleboard, it's everything you'd ever want if you were lost along the vastness of San Pablo Avenue.

Ivy Room   858 San Pablo Ave., Albany, 510-524-9220

The Ivy's is a fine little place for those who can't decide whether they like dives with character or music venues masquerading as lowbrow bars. Mellow and crotchety during the day, the Ivy hosts live music several nights a week. It's one of the best places to catch up-and-comers in the Bay Area. The jukebox alone is well worth the trek.

Mallard Club   752 San Pablo Ave., Albany, 510-524-8450

The Mallard brings together Berkeley graduate students, Albany locals, and the occasional spillover from bad music night at the Ivy Room across the street. It's a friendly place with a dedicated following, lots of history, and an outdoor patio.

The Ruby Room   132 14th St., Oakland, 510-444-7224

If this place were in San Francisco, it would be pack in the hipsters and pour weak and overpriced drinks. Well, it's got the hipsters, but the drinks are cheap and honestly poured. The dark, reddish tint of the bar screams of something from another era, but at heart, the Ruby Room's just a dreamy little stop on Oakland's downtown drinking circuit.

Smitty's Cocktails   3339 Grand Ave., Oakland, 510-834-1591

Esteemed drinking pal Boris swears that Smitty's was one of his favorite hang-outs during his Oakland years. My time there has been limited, but the place does have a retro old neon sign, cheap pool, shuffleboard, and most impor-tantly, affordable drinks, which gets it in my book, any day.

SOUTH BAY

Antonio's Nut House
321 California, Palo Alto, 650-321-2550

Some call this ever-packed place the only real dive in Silicon Valley. While that's not the opinion of this drinker, Antonio's is still a great place to settle down for cheap beer and peanuts (which come courtesy of a stuffed gorilla).

Black Watch   141 1/2 N. Santa Cruz Ave., Los Gatos, 408-354-2200

A dive four decades in the making, Black Watch is a favorite among dart fanatics and seekers of the perfect (and seemingly bottomless) kamikaze. Weekends the place can be overrun with Saturday-afternoon bikers and Saturday night partiers.

Caravan   98 S. Almaden Ave., San Jose, 408-995-6220

Grizzled regulars, failed dot-commers, and lost Greyhound riders are among the cast at this fabled downtown San Jose dive. Richer times seemed to be pushing the place in less divey directions, but thankfully, times have changed and the Caravan is back to its old glory.

Cinebar   69 E. San Fernando St., San Jose, 408-971-0209

Regulars mourned the passing of former bartender/proprietor Ace, and they some-times raise a toast toward the disco ball in his honor. A good stop on San Jose's downtown bar circuit, Cinebar can become packed with college kids on weekends.

Paul & Eddie's   21619 Stevens Creek Blvd., Cupertino, 408-252-2226

Cupertino's longtime local's bar is a fine place to while away a few hours, or a lifetime, over cheap drinks, cheaper pool, and free popcorn. Taxidermy fans will enjoy the gallery of dead stuff on the walls; but most folks just watch TV.

NORTH BAY

The Silver Peso   450 Magnolia Ave., Larkspur, 415-924-3448

Marin County may have sprouted fancy everywhere else, but the Peso is still the good old Peso. Cheap drafts, lopsided shuffleboard, and tilted floorboards. While it's no longer the biker bar it once was, it still draws some crusty elements as well as your standard Marin folks.